THE ART OF MIXING WORK AND PLAY

By
STEVE WILSON
Psychologist and THE JOYOLOGIST

Illustrations by
MICHAEL SENETT

APPLIED HUMOR SYSTEMS
® 1992

Printed on recycled paper.

ISBN: 089894-052-4

Cover Design: Michael Senett
Book Design: Michael Senett
Cartoon Illustration: Michael Senett

10 9 8 7 6 5 4 3 2 1

Printed in the United States

Advocate Publishing Group

"Once I lovingly began to pay careful attention to what made me most happy, I came to realize that freely living my life had nothing to do with whether I was defying or complying with authority. Gradually, I lost interest in the distinction between work and play and set out instead to take charge of my life by spending as much of my time as possible doing those things that I find personally meaningful, either alone or in the company of people who matter to me.

"That inner power has far less to do with pleasing the powerful or impressing the powerless than it does with doing as I please. It depends more on experiencing my input than on displaying my output. I'm learning to work playfully and to play hard. After all these years, I believe I'm beginning to get the hang of it."

Sheldon Kopp ("Rock, Paper, Scissors," CompCare, 1989).

DEDICATION

For three men who have my deepest appreciation, respect, admiration, and gratitude:

Norman Cousins

William J. "Bill" McGrane

and my father, Jack Wilson

ACKNOWLEDGEMENTS

Thanks to my wife, Pam, whose steadfast encouragement and unrelenting affection erases any of my doubts, and who is soft, smart, tough, and cuddly. What more could a man want?

Thanks to my stepmother, Helen Wilson, who understands and teaches the value of laughter and positive attitude.

Thanks to my father, Jack Wilson, for the lion's share of my sense of humor, and for his shining example of courage and integrity.

Thanks to my sister, Phyllis Torner, who has inspired us and shown us all how important it is to wake up and smell the coffee.

Thanks to my children: Shawn, Jenifer, Rachel, Josh, and Bethany, who motivate me with their love and their jokes and their laughter and their need for food, clothing, shelter, and tuition.

Thanks to Jeff Kuhn, who took a shot at being a humorist's apprentice and became the inventive and persevering backbone of the research for this volume.

Thanks to Ginney Duncan, Client Services Coordinator at Ohio Professional Counseling Services, for typing, collating, copying, copying, copying, and for her keenly supportive sense of the ironic.

Thanks to Rita Milios and Helene Ayers for making me look good by their superb editing.

Thanks to Wayne Hill for years of friendships and support, hours of brainstorming, moments of inspired insight, and a few fleeting seconds that one time when he actually considered paying for breakfast.

Thanks to Michael Senett, talented genius of form, space, color, and design, and humorous perspective, whose inspired cartoons and illustrations light up this book from cover to cover.

Thanks to Steve White, publisher par excellence, whose wizardry transforms ideas into books, and makes it look easy.

Thanks to the thousands of Humor Pen Pals, participants in my humor workshops, and readers of THE STEVE WILSON REPORT all across North America who shared their experiences and encouragement about mixing work and play.

S.W.

SALUTE

The preeminent author, scholar, and teacher, Joseph Campbell, said that there is a threat to our lives today that we all face. "Is the system going to flatten you out and deny you your humanity," he asked, "or are you going to be able to make use of the system to the attainment of human purposes?" He wanted us to think about how we could relate to a system "so that you are not compulsively serving it." How are you going to "live in your period of history as a human being?" He answered, "By holding to your own ideals for yourself and, like Luke Skywalker, rejecting the system's impersonal claims upon you."

Many of the people who attend my humor seminars have observed that those who most need the information will probably never read this kind of book. However, I believe that there are people who need this book even more than those who will not read it: those who have to work with those who will not read it.

Therefore, let us salute those employees everywhere who do a better job, and do everyone else a favor, because they bring an element of playfulness to work. Like Luke Skywalker, they hold to their own ideals, their sense of humanity, often in the face of a system that has become numb to the pain of its stressful and dangerous workplaces. They help us to keep our balance, sanity, health, and our humanity.

# # #

"Humor is ubiquitous because it is a survival mechanism in this 'vale of tears'. It is the healing balm that encourages us to right the innumerable wrongs that still exist in the world for which we have fundamental responsibilities." --Marvin R. Koller, Professor of Sociology, Kent (Ohio) State University

"THE ART OF MIXING WORK AND PLAY"
(PWLOARYK)

By Steve Wilson, Psychologist

TABLE OF CONTENTS

FOREWORD

HUMOR AND SELF-ESTEEM: HONORING YOUR INCARNATION AND BECOMING JOYFUL AND EFFECTIVE IN THE 90s

"But each incarnation, you might say, has a potentiality, and the mission of life is to live that potentiality. How do you do it? My answer is, 'Follow your bliss'."

--Joseph Campbell

This is a serious book about some powerful aspects of the human condition which happen to be fun: laughter, playfulness, and humor. Throughout the book I refer to these as your birthright. By this I mean that laughter and play are abilities with which you are naturally endowed at your creation. Laughter and play are vital to your survival in good health and an absolute requisite for your maximum appreciation and enjoyment of your life.

In treating many patients, I have had many opportunities to observe various kinds of dis-ease that arise in personality development. Men and women, and their children, come for help because of a variety of problems: depression, anxiety, panic attacks; faltering, failing, and failed relationships; ruptures in family systems; addictions and compulsive disorders; death, divorce, suicide, abandonment; life-threatening illness; job dissatisfaction and career uncertainty. They are experiencing a painful absence of peace of mind, joy, and the ability to effectively manage their lives and the problems that confront them.

A great deal has been written recently about important contemporary ideas concerning personality development. Some of the people charting this new course are Robert Bly, John Bradshaw, Janet Woititz, Terry Kellogg, Janet Black, and Pia Mellody. In recent years, significant work has been done in the formulation of an understanding of how we become either joyful or unhappy adults. Unhappy adults will act out their misery by abusing their children, becoming addicted, becoming mentally or physically ill, failing at intimacy, being unhappy at work, or making themselves and others miserable.

Mixing work and play, having fun at work, promoting laughter in the workplace, and enjoying work have a direct relation to becoming an effective and joyful adult. Avoiding or suppressing PWLOARYK (P-L-A-Y and W-O-R-K) or doing it the wrong way reflects mistaken beliefs and unhealthy attitudes. These attitudes develop in childhood through a specific set of dynamics in families and society--a chain of events we can describe, understand, and overcome.

SENSE OF HUMOR ABUSE

Misconceptions about laughter and play have become incorporated into child-rearing practices. The roots of distorted concepts of reality and damaged self esteem reach down into attitudes about laughter and play that some parents hold, and then transfer to their children. In spite of the fact that many of the ideas and practices may be wide-spread, and are considered within parents' rights and responsibilities, they do not help children become effective and joyful adults.

I am amazed and saddened, but not surprised, by the responses I receive when I ask the participants in my humor workshops for examples of the criticisms to which they were subjected, as children, for laughing. I consider the giving of demeaning and false information to be a specific form of intellectual and emotional abuse which can be called *sense of humor abuse*. These attitudes, even though they may be unintentionally transferred, once inculcated in children, foster dysfunction. When the children become adults, they bring those dysfunctional attitudes with them into the workplace.

Some children are told, "Laugh and the world laughs with you, cry and you cry alone." This idea puts a higher value on pleasant rather than unpleasant emotions and reactions. In reality, all emotions have value. Why should we be isolated--shunned or alone--for crying? If you believed this proverb, you would inhibit crying, and thereby lose touch with a significant component of emotional health. The same problem arises when laughing is criticized or put down. In some families, the joyful noise of laughter, the natural sound of playfulness, is not permitted. In these families we often find that one or both of the parents had been abused as a child, or is addicted, chronically physically ill, mentally ill, or codependent. Some children are abused by being "shushed" and shamed; some are hit, sent away to their rooms or out of the house, or screamed at for laughing. Some children's intelligence and creativity are attacked, or they are otherwise punished for engaging in the laughter, play, and humor that is appropriate and healthy for their age level.

Sense of humor abuse occurs when erroneous or superstitious information is passed on in a way that frightens children or makes them feel bad about themselves. Phrases such as the following are familiar refrains. "Laugh before breakfast and you will cry before supper." "Don't laugh so hard, you'll have a nervous breakdown." "No one likes a person who laughs too much." "When you laugh you sound like a whore with a cold." "You laugh like a horse." "What an awful cackle." "That's a horrible guffaw." "You laugh too loud." "You squeal when you laugh." "You always laugh at the wrong time." "You laugh at everything." "How can you laugh when there is so much sadness in the world?" "Laughing can make you throw up." "You could hurt yourself from laughing so much." And the fatal, but entirely false, "You could die from laughing." The self-conscious inhibitions and diminished self-esteem created in children by such statements, especially when they come from trusted adults, may persist for a lifetime, and can play a significant part in adult dis-ease and dysfunction.

The principles for mixing work and play are based on respecting the value and vulnerability of all people. They are principles that can be used by anyone to help recover from the damaging effects of sense of humor abuse during their childhood. And, by becoming aware of the true importance of humor, laughter, and play to human existence, we can better protect ourselves--mentally, emotionally, physically, and spiritually--especially at work, and continue to become effective and joyful.

LAUGHTER, PLAY, DEVELOPMENT, AND SURVIVAL

Laughter and play are fundamentally necessary for successful human development and for the maintenance of physical and emotional health throughout one's lifetime. The significant role of childhood playfulness for healthy human development has long been substantiated, underscoring the tragedy of one of the typical effects of living in a dysfunctional family, a condition known as *the loss of a carefree childhood*. Michael S. Duchowny, University of Miami School of Medicine, reports that the brain substrates for laughter are fully functional at birth. He says that ". . . the brain mechanisms for participating in laughter are of special importance, possibly because these pathways are closely involved with processes necessary for the organism's survival." The ability to laugh and smile is virtually inborn in human beings, and it is vital. Laughter and play are

natural ways of learning about our world and responding to it. Human beings are the only creatures on earth that can laugh and smile (you may think your dog or cat is smiling at you, but as far as we know, only human beings have a *sense of humor*). Humor helps us to stay in touch with our true higher power, and that spiritual connection has enormous survival value in times of trouble. Perhaps this is why it is said that laughter is *God's gift to mankind.*

Laughter and play are our natural birthright, vital, necessary, and part of every human being's intrinsic authenticity.

These concepts have provided powerful tools not only for my work in private practice but for my lectures and seminars. More than ever, I see extraordinary results as adults use these insights to become effective and joyful at work and in their personal lives.

What makes this information difficult to grasp is the fact that many of the characteristics our society has traditionally valued as desirable are really unhealthy. Pia Mellody, author and nationally recognized authority on codependence, in her significant book, *FACING CODEPENDENCE* (Harper & Row), points out, "Our society believes that people who exhibit the characteristics (of codependence) at one extreme--arrogance, invulnerability, perfectionism, antidependence, and 'being in control'--are healthy, well-adjusted adults. However, the pain in their lives from unfulfilling relationships, unsatisfying careers, depression, and other problems would indicate that they are *not* functional adults." They are suffering from codependence, a condition estimated to affect 96% of Americans.

Suppressing healthy humor, laughter, and play anywhere, including at work, is a denial of the authentic nature of a human being. Mellody has constructed a model of human development that provides a basis for understanding who we are, what we need, and how to recover from not getting what we really needed as children.

A FRAMEWORK FOR HONORING HUMAN BEING

A basic premise of Mellody's model is that all human beings are born with certain conditions in common. We all begin life vulnerable, valuable, imperfect, dependent, and immature (and, I would add, able to laugh and smile and needing to play). These natural characteristics make us human beings. "Functional parents," says Mellody, "help their children develop each separate characteristic properly, so that they arrive in adulthood as mature, functional adults who feel good about themselves."

A functional adult is one who experiences adequate levels of self-esteem, is vulnerable, but can establish boundaries for self-protection without harming others, is imperfect, accountable for imperfections and spiritual, is able to be interdependent (intimate) and able to get needs and wants met appropriately, and is mature at an age level. A functional adult is capable of integrating work and play in a way that enhances his or her effectiveness and joy without bringing harmful consequences to others. It has been said that "what soap is to the body, laughter is to the soul." To deny laughter is to deny one's spiritual endowment, prohibit a cleansing of the soul, and prevent maturation into the experience of a fully effective and joyful adult life.

It is the role of parents and others engaged to influence the development of children to acknowledge the child's needs in a responsible way, providing guidance without shaming. It is out of such a responsible, non-shaming structure that the child can learn to be an effective and joyful adult, able to protect him or her self from intrusion on his or her body, thoughts, feelings, and actions; able to negotiate to meet his or her needs; able to experience adequate self-esteem, capable of authentic intimacy, of being non-offensive to others, spiritually connected, able to express their own reality in moderation. Out of such a structure comes an adult who counts humor and fun as being of significant importance, and is able to engage in guilt-free pleasure, laugh spontaneously, and mix work and play effectively.

HUMOR AND AUTHENTICITY

We are born *vulnerable.* We need protection and we need to learn how to protect ourselves without offending others. A good sense of humor is part of our psychological and physiological protection. Humor and laughter help us keep a balanced perspective on our reality and help us to face and cope with difficult or painful reality through truth that can be told in humor. Humor is the spoonful of sugar that helps the medicine go down. True mirthful laughter affects every system in the body in a healthful way. Laughter and good humor benefits the cardiovascular system, provides respiratory therapy, activation of the immune system, muscle relaxation, pain relief, and improves digestion. Suppressing humor deprives one of these advantages.

An enormous amount of information has been published that warns us about the ill effects of stress. Along the way in this book I will describe research findings which give evidence that an effective way to manage stress is through humor. I have observed that many people have a desk drawer at work which contains a number of drug store remedies for the ill effects of stress--Tums, Maalox, Mylanta, Excedrine, Valium, Xanex, and Kaopectate. There is reason to believe that "humor first-aid" is so effective in preventing the ill effects of stress that it could eliminate the need for chemical remedies.

In his last book, *HEAD FIRST: THE BIOLOGY OF HOPE* (Dutton), Norman Cousins said, ". . .I learned that it is not unscientific to talk about a biology of hope—or of any of the positive emotions . . . hope, faith, love, will to live, festivity, playfulness, purpose, and determination—are powerful bio-chemical prescriptions." Josh Billings is often quoted as having said, "There ain't much fun in medicine, but there's a heck of a lot of medicine in fun," and the bible instructs us that "a merry heart doeth good like a medicine." Now, thanks to the substantial research which has been promoted by Cousins and others, we know these words are valid.

We are born *valuable*. We are products of the highest intelligence in the universe and we are, therefore, all equally worthy of the highest value. Our value is inherent in our *being*, as opposed to our *doing*. Our society confuses these values and leads us to the erroneous belief that self-esteem will be derived from accomplishments and achievements such as grades in school, job titles, and material wealth. Striving for this false sense of esteem has turned many people into *human doings* who lose touch with their authentic *human being*. Without proper ways to measure our worth, we feel either inferior (less-than) or superior (more-than) rather than equal to others. This gives rise to negative, hurtful humor: racist, sexist, put-down jokes; humor that disparages another's natural endowments, and beliefs, or emphasizes imperfections. Functional adults engage in positive humor that lifts others up, is good-hearted, and values individual differences.

Joel Goodman, Ed.D., is director of the Humor Project in Saratoga Springs, New York. I am deeply indebted to him for introducing me to the power of a *value-based* approach to humor. In *THE HANDBOOK OF HUMOR RESEARCH, VOL. II* (Springer-Verlag), he says, "Humor is laughter made from pain—not pain inflicted by laughter. If we can interrupt and help others become aware of destructive humor patterns, and if we can replace these with positive, nourishing humor models, the sensitivity to humor will lead to more effective and appropriate sense of humor . . . an approach to life to help you feel *more* connected with others, to help *you* feel *more* self-esteem . . ."

We are born *imperfect*. No matter how well we learn to manage our lives, we never can achieve perfection. We all make mistakes. But functional adults do not strive for perfection, and they have a good-natured acceptance of their own and other's imperfection. Much humor arises from our imperfection. Steve Allen said, "There's nothing quite so funny as the unintended humor of reality." *Candid Camera* and other blooper shows on radio and TV have been extraordinarily popular because they "catch us in the act of being ourselves" and, through laughter, give us a chance to accept our authenticity. Not allowing laughter and play at work can create an unrealistic expectation of perfect performance which sets up anxiety, fear, and stress. Mixing work and play creates a relaxed atmosphere which acknowledges our authenticity and actually enables us to be more effective and productive and fosters higher morale.

Can you take yourself lightly? Even in the midst of some "serious" task you might make a mistake that has humorous proportions. Here are a few examples of unintended humor produced by the reality of everyday life. A student's view of history: "Abraham Lincoln's mother died in infancy, and he was born in a log cabin which he built with his own hands." A claimant filling in an automobile insurance report: "I pulled away from the side of the road, glanced at my mother-in-law, and headed over the embankment." From a church bulletin board: "Wednesday the Ladies Literary Society will meet. Mrs. Johnson will sing 'Put Me In My Little Bed,' accompanied by the reverend." A physician noted in a patient's record: "This mother of a 2-year-old desires a circumcision." A sign seen in an Acapulco restaurant: "The manager has personally passed all the water served here." Self-esteem is related to the ability to be kind-hearted toward our own human errors.

We are born *dependent*. We have needs and wants that we cannot meet alone. We require the help of others. This dependence will remain all through our lives. No matter how independent we think we are, we can never satisfy all of our needs and wants without sometimes turning to others for help. Not to be able to ask for help, or to feel ashamed to need help, are dysfunctional (antidependent). Functional adults can ask for help without feeling "less-than" other people. Good humor and play at work breaks down the barriers between people and opens up communication. People who laugh together work together better. Healthy humor promotes teamwork, teamplay and effective cooperation.

We are born *immature*. We do not express our reality moderately. We cry and tantrum, we laugh and giggle hysterically. Dysfunctional adults continue to have difficulty expressing their reality in moderation. They ignore or are out of touch with certain needs, wants, and emotions, or they are overwhelmed by them. Functional adults are able to be moderate about the same things that create chaos, disharmony, and pain for the dysfunctional adult. We all retain an element of the child in us. If our inner child is wounded, we are afraid to laugh and play fearing we will be punished, and we try to stop others from laughing and playing, too. If our inner child is wounded, we tend to use hostile or sarcastic humor to hurt others (to boost our own sagging self-esteem); we tend to use humor at inappropriate times, and without sensitivity to others.

The dysfunctional adult uses humor, laughter, and play too much, too little, or at the wrong times and in the wrong places, and experiences many "backfires." The functional adult is able to manage laughter and play in moderation and derives great benefits for himself or herself and those with whom he or she works. Functional adults savor their "free time," take vacations, engage in celebration and festivity. They take time to play with their children, provide attitudinal balance in their workplaces, and are better lovers because they are not afraid of looking foolish. Functional adults experience greater personal satisfaction with life.

HONORING YOUR INCARNATION AT WORK

At work, we may be attacked by demanding and complaining customers (and co-workers, too, at times), deadlines, financial pres-

customers (and co-workers, too, at times), deadlines, financial pressures, competition, and a myriad of things that can go wrong every day. The concepts and principles presented in this book show how mixing work and play in functional, healthy ways—that acknowledge, respect, and embrace our authenticity as human beings—will help to protect us, and increase our effectiveness, satisfaction, productivity, and joy.

# # #

CHAPTER 1

GOOD-BYE ROLEX, HELLO, MICKEY MOUSE: THE GRINNING OF AMERICA

"Choose a job you love, and you will never have to work a day in your life." --Confucius

"Among the chief worries of today's executives is the large number of unemployed still on the payrolls" --Anonymous

"Work is the crabgrass in the lawn of life." --Bored Employee

THE NEW WAY OF THINKING ABOUT WORK

Do you remember your first box of Crayola crayons? More than just about anything, I wanted the giant box of (WOW!) 48 colors. What I remember most about my crayons is the waxy aroma and how the paper wrappers felt scratchy on my fingers. (Tests reveal that the smell of Crayola crayons is one of the 20 most recognizable odors to American adults.) I remember coloring books (stay inside the lines) and coloring green grass, yellow suns, purple cows, *red* hair. Did you know that many of the most successful people started out early in life with a box of Crayola crayons?

Crayola crayons have evolved and changed since they were first introduced almost ninety years ago. And the company now produces a complete line of creative expression products. But if you watch the face of a child playing with Crayola crayons for the first time, you know that these slender, magical sticks of color are just as wondrous and important as ever.

Where do Crayola crayons come from? Who is responsible for all this magic? They are manufactured by Binney & Smith of Easton, Pennsylvania. The company has produced products for the classroom since 1903, when the nickel eight-crayon box first appeared. They have not done at all badly. But, between 1984 and 1990 under the leadership of its new president, Richard S. Gurin, sales jumped 92% to $240 million. What could have accounted for so much growth? According to an Associated Press report, it is Gurin's philosophy that is in large part responsible for Binney & Smith making its mark in the world of business.

It is fascinating that a company that has had such phenomenal success is led by a man who espouses a *conscious fun philosophy*. Asked what the secret is, Gurin said, "We're focused on fun and profit, and know that the two go together." He gives his employees this formula: "If we are not making a lot of money, we won't be having a lot of fun. And if we're not having fun, we're probably just not making enough money."

This philosophy represents a remarkable shift in thinking about work. Large and growing numbers of people are changing the way they feel about work and what they want from it. The up-to-now insatiable, consuming baby-boomers are changing their minds about work.

William Broyles, Jr., had been editor in chief of *Newsweek* before he wrote in Esquire about the emptiness of success: "Each morning I struggled into my suit, picked up my briefcase, went to my glamorous job, and died a little." He said that he realized that, in his search for satisfaction through success, he had "climbed the wrong mountain, and the only thing to do was go down and climb another one."

The striving, upwardly mobile managers and executives who are shaping the workplace now and for the future are, literally and figuratively, sick and tired. They realize that achievement and power are not synonymous with joy. They are changing their minds about their work and their life values. They have come to realize the price they pay for viewing work as only a laborious, torturous drudge or a means to materialistic ends. There is a growing chorus echoing in the refrain, "Stop! I don't want to have it all. What is it worth?"

Amy Saltzman, in her book, *Downshifting* (HarperCollins), described a trend in which people are "easing back on work in the interest of moving ahead in life." She defined five types of downshifting—ways to escape the rat-race—that included refusing promotions that would require greater responsibility or energy, moving to a less-demanding career, starting your own business, and moving from the city to the country. How many people are really in a position to make such changes? Mary Lynne Musgrove, a Columbus, Ohio, career counselor said that, in her practice, she saw more yearning for downshifting than actual enactment. Downshifting by moving out does not appear to be a reasonable option for most employees. How many workers can, like Broyles, climb down off the mountain altogether and climb up another?

San Francisco attorney Richard Such would like to see a legislative mandate for a six-week vacation for certain workers. The practice is already in effect in Germany, France, Italy, Great Britain, and Sweden (where workers get up to eight weeks vacation). What is the likelihood that such a law could be passed in time for you to enjoy the extra time off? Not too great. Indeed, at present, a lack of evidence on the matter, makes any productivity benefits from longer vacations questionable.

But, because "happiness is an inside job," there is a way to change things at the workplace to achieve what might be called "in-house downshifting." It is called PWLOARYK, the art of mixing work and play.

Most people enviously consider work to be fun only for a lucky few. But, any successful business person will tell you that what appears to many to be luck is really the result of persistent, intelligent effort. Therefore, anyone who is willing to make the effort can have this kind of "luck." They can find opportunities to make work fun. This attitude, translated into practice in the right way, is proving to be a significant contributing factor to the success and profitability of some American businesses.

There now exist many examples of corporations that make "fun" one of their top priorities by including it in their stated goals. For example, Karen Kapusta, Director of Vision Effectiveness for Coors Ceramics Co., shared their VISION STATEMENT about putting humor to work at work. Their statement is clear and strong. It emphasizes unparalleled quality, unprecedented service, and heart-felt commitment. It contains this sentence: "Our work is fun and rewarding."

Companies that adopt this kind of philosophy about fun experience dramatic decreases in reject rates, turnover, and healthcare costs with corresponding increases in overall sales and after-tax profit. Among the corporations reaping these benefits are North American Tool & Die, Dreyer's Grand Ice Cream, W.L. Gore & Associates, Tandem Computer, and Domino's Pizza. And while the statistics are, of course, most impressive in the large corporations, the same concept of mixing work and play applies, with resounding success, to small businesses, too.

Some years ago I came across an impressive statistic related to the business world: a fifteen percent increase in morale can account for as much as a forty percent increase in productivity. This doesn't surprise me. And, it seems quite likely that this same estimate probably holds true for work done at home and in our personal lives, too.

Today's laboring workforce continues under the often oppressive influence of the ethics of the puritan influence that was brought to this country more than 500 years ago. Simply stated, according to this strict dogma, work is exalted and amusement is forbidden. This idea persists today, and is being used to justify attitudes and business practices that many believe to be unhealthy and counter-productive. Anatomically stated, toiling under the predominant work ethic twists workers into pretzels as we attempt to obey such commands as: "shoulder to the wheel, nose to the grindstone, put your back into it, best foot forward, toe the line, chin up, stiff upper lip, keep your eye on the goal, ear to the ground, get a leg up, lend a hand, plenty of backbone, bite the bullet, guts and glory, and at the same time, cover your ass." From this awkward position, who could work with optimum efficiency and productivity?

SICK AND TIRED OF BEING SICK AND TIRED

As a result of the universal application of this work ethic for the 150 years since the Industrial Revolution, people suffer from far too many muscle spasms, migraines, ulcers (women are now equal to men in the rate of peptic ulcers), chest pains, and coronaries (the rate of heart attack among women increased 100% over the last twenty years). We face skyrocketing healthcare costs and injured-worker claims, not to mention premature death.

But there is a movement calling for a new way of defining and carrying out work. When we were young we all heard the proverbial warning that all work and no play would make Jack a dull, if not downright sick, boy (and it is obviously none too good for Jane, either). Apparently the baby-boomers (and many of the more seasoned managers) have heard the warning. They ignored it for a long time, but now many of them are taking heed of Lily Tomlin's observation that the trouble with the rat race is that, even if you win, you're still a rat! Many

of us want to change our workstyle. We know that in a world that is ever faster spinning out of control, if we are going to regain control and save our sanity and our lives, we must restore balance to every aspect of our living.

Ron Zemke, senior editor of *TRAINING* magazine, describes the changes this way: "Out are: conspicuous consumption, greed, self-aggrandizement and 20-hour-a-day careerism. Adios, Beamers and Rolexes. Farewell, furs and diamonds and designer originals. Bye-bye, braces, bow ties, hyperthyroid titles and inflated paychecks. So long Lee Iacocca and Steven Jobs. In are: frugality, value, greening, charitable instincts, introspection, self-doubt, and evenings at home with family and friends. Hello, K-Mart and Sears, Bean and Land's End, tithing and good works. Hello, making ends meet and doing without. Hello, pleasant jobs and being a part of something worthy. Hello, Scrabble."

Zemke reminds us of a fundamental truth: "It's time to put some living back into life. There is more to 'being' than worrying about 'six sigma' quality and niche markets and one's position in the hierarchy of replaceable cogs in a commercial machine." We have already heard the first rumblings of this shift in values. It is moving at an accelerating pace and will be roaring down the pike at us any minute. We will enter the millennium with a different way of looking at work. We will re-define "work." We will need guidelines for operating under the definition. This book provides some of these guidelines--the ones that are the most fun.

WORK WONT ALWAYS BE WORK

We already know that not all work takes place in an environment of paid employment. We work in our gardens, work on our cars, work on our hobbies, work at our golf and tennis games. We do housework, community work, and church work. We work on our marriages, and do the work of raising a family. So, paid or not, just when is work work? It seems that one of the main determining factors of whether or not we view an activity as "work" has a lot to do with how we look at a task, how much pleasure and satisfaction it brings us, how much "fun" it is for us. Tom Sawyer convinced his pals that white-washing a fence was not work at all, and so got them to do it for him. Was it work? Tom said, "Maybe it is and maybe it ain't . . . all I know is it suits Tom Sawyer." When we can make work more fun--paid or not--more people will gladly do more of it.

PLAY IMPROVES MORALE AND PRODUCTIVITY

According to management consultant, Fred Pryor, "Humor is good for your health and that of your employees. Healthy, happy employees are on the job. Unhappy ones tend to call in 'sick' - and they may well be." In many cases they may only be sick of work! Noted author and

management expert Tom Peters observes, "In general, a spirited environment is marked by laughter--enthusiasm for being on a team and trying darn near anything to make the service or product better." Business consultant and psychologist, Bruce E. Roselle contends that managers and others must be trained to have more job enjoyment to keep them motivated and content. He says, "Those who play in their work are the ones who perform closest to their peak level, they are the ones to be taken most seriously."

Traditionally, work and play are thought of as separate and opposite activities. Pryor points out that many workers feel self-conscious about being playful on the job "and many supervisors feel obliged to discourage playing at work." John Bowman is a sociologist who questions the usual way we look at work and play. He has collected numerous examples of occasions when "work activities are accomplished quite playfully." He has gathered evidence that "playful activities either relieved tension, made very boring work more tolerable, or built solidarity among a group of employees." Too many supervisors are afraid that fun is wasteful. Imagine how much more they could accomplish if they realized that there are clearly times when fun and playfulness are the most economical approaches to work. Dr. Gerald H. Graham, editor of *Applied Management Newsletter*, suggests, "If your department has engaged in fewer than four fun kinds of activities during the past three months, you might want to consider ways of adding fun to your work environment." That is what this book is about.

SIX QUESTIONS, THREE PREMISES TO HELP YOU BRING WORK AND PLAY TOGETHER

This book answers six questions:

1. What do we mean when we use works like "humor" and "fun"?
2. Can a sense of humor or a sense of fun be acquired?
3. Can work and play be combined?
4. Can play be combined with other aspects of life?
5. If so, why bother?
6. If it is worth the bother, how do you do it?

To find the answers, I have read the extensive literature on the subject, including humorous works, scientific research, news reports, poetry and philosophy; I have interviewed numerous people (obscure, celebrated, educated, talented, and ordinary); and, I have spent thousands of hours with patients in my practice of psychotherapy, and with the more than 90,000 people who have attended my programs, speeches, seminars, and workshops. All of this has led me to three important premises.

PREMISE #1: There is a "sense of humor continuum."

There is a wide variation in the degree to which people have a sense of humor. For the sake of discussion, it is helpful to divide people into three categories. We can say that, when it comes to humor, there are three kinds of people: Humor Impaired, Humor Accidental, and Humor Powered.

PREMISE #2: There are certain principles which anyone can use to combine work and play, become Humor Powered and get the most out of life.

These are proved psychological principles, not very well-known until now. Everyone can use these principles, and become Humor Powered.

PREMISE #3: Everyone can locate and develop their sense of humor and sense of fun.

It is possible to make sense out of humor, but a sense of humor is not acquired by luck or genetics. It is something that must be developed; but everyone can do it.

A NEW JARGON

As you may have already figured out, the term PWLOARYK is actually the interweaving of P-L-A-Y and W-O-R-K to achieve a graphic and literal representation of the art of mixing work and play. Research data and reports of observations on the validity of this concept are very promising. And yet, noticeably missing from the language of management and the psychology of organizational development are words that quickly and easily define the concept. It seemed to me that an important contribution to this research would be to develop a fitting new vocabulary. I therefore introduce *Pwloaryk* as the first word in the new vocabulary of mixing work and play.

DEFINITION AND USAGE:

1. **pwloaryk** \pw-lor-ik\ *n.* The art of mixing work and play; finding ways to add humor or any other positive interaction or experience to activities usually known as "work" which, in turn, enhance the psychological health and/or productivity of individuals and work groups. Example: "We sure could use more pwloaryk around here."

2. **pwloarykist** *n.* One that specializes in the art of mixing work and play. Example: "Thank heavens our boss is an expert pwloarykist."

3. **pwloarykable** *adj.* One who, or that which, is worthy of mixing play into work, esp. as being uncommon or extraordinary. Example: "Installing a hot-tub in the employee's lounge is a pwloarykable idea!"

4. **pwloarykally** *adv.* Example: "We get a lot more accomplished since we learned how to do things pwloarykally."

5. **pwloarykabonga** *tnage. mut. ninj. turtl.* Example: "Listen to the laughter coming from our top-notch sales department. Pwloarykabonga, dudes!"

ARE YOU HUMOR IMPAIRED, POWERFUL, OR ACCIDENTAL?

You probably have noticed some people, more than others, seem to be jolly and up-beat and able to laugh at life's little—and sometimes even larger—problems. Then there are people who laugh only at their own jokes. "They," according to humorist Dale Irvin, "are called brothers-in-law." Some people are happy and enthusiastic even when things don't go right. Some people have an easy laugh and a ready smile; we say they are "warm" and "inviting". Some people are relaxed and in good humor so much of the time that they are a joy to be with and to work with; everyone wants to be on their team. You may have wondered how they do it.

There is no generally accepted scientific test for one's sense of humor; researchers in this area vary in their ideas of what a sense of humor is and how to measure it. However, it is helpful to think of the

humor is and how to measure it. However, it is helpful to think of the sense of humor as measurable along a continuum. At one end of the continuum one finds the Humor Impaired. I sometimes use an abbreviation and call this group "himps". These are the people who never seem to get the joke, never understand what is funny about everyday situations, and don't laugh or smile or do things just for fun very often. We experience them as grim, overly serious, or "negative" people, and find them as our co-workers, bosses, and right in our own families. Based on my experiences, I would estimate that the Humor Impaired account for 15-20% of the general population.

At the other end of the continuum are the Humor Powered people. These are people who understand and appreciate humor and treat it as a valuable resource. We experience them as warm, easy going, balanced, and "positive". They smile and laugh easily. They use humor consciously, competently, and confidently. Again, based on my experience, I would estimate that Humor Powered people account for about 15% of the population.

In the middle of the sense of humor continuum are the remaining 65-70% of people who are Humor Accidental. These people laugh at other people's jokes, have their favorite comedians, sitcoms, and comic strips, and will occasionally choose a comedy when they go to the movies. They get some of the benefits of humor and are not too difficult to getalong with, but they are not getting the most out of life. Fortunately, PWLOARYK is possible for everyone!

HUMOR VARIATIONS

Some humor is hostile, offensive, hurtful, and a turn-off; it backfires. Some people can't remember a joke to save their lives, or they tell it terribly, or at the wrong time. Some people are dreadfully cheerful, harping at us to "smile" and "cheer up." Some people are just plain grim; dull, boring, solemn, stiff, and generally un-amused. They don't "get the joke" and they keep urging us to get back to work, reminding us, "We're not here to have fun!"

Some humor happens spontaneously. Some humor happens accidentally. Some humor is well-planned. Some humor is "just what we needed" to break tension and bring relief. Some people are good at telling humorous stories to warm up audiences or put customers in a more receptive frame of mind.

A few people (Himps) just dont seem to have much of a sense of humor at all and they are most likely to reject PWLOARYK as an idea of fun. Most people (Humor Accidental) have some humor in their lives sometimes, which is helpful, but not particularly powerful. And then there are some people who seem to have good, powerful humor working for them all the time. These are Humor Powered people, and it is within this group that we will probably find most of the PWLOARYKists.

Humor Powered people are those who, on a daily basis, are able to capitalize on the benefits of humor. They use humor to make their work lighter and healthier, they have a better "bottom-line," and they enjoy life more. They seem to have a greater abundance of laughter, play, pleasure, creativity, festivity, frivolity, and joy. They seem to know something that the others don't, and they are putting it to good use in every aspect of their lives. With the help of this book, you can be that way, too!

IS THERE A "HUMOROUS PERSONALITY"?

There probably is not a single personality type that can claim all the humor. Researchers have studied the personality characteristics of "fun" people, people with a good sense of humor. They wanted to find out, besides humor, what other personality characteristics are likely to be found in a person who is said to have a good sense of humor. In other words, what are the personality traits and characteristics of 'fun' people? The findings of several researchers are similar. When we think of 'fun people' we are likely to imagine:

Sense of humor
Not always serious
Intelligent

Energetic
Hardworking
Can laugh at themselves
Outgoing
Friendly
Competent.

Management professor David Abramis, concludes, "Notice that these are characteristics of people you'd probably like to hire, even if your goal was not to have fun." These are characteristics you would find attractive and would want in a friend or mate or neighbor, or anyone with whom you do business. And Dr. Abramis has numerous specific examples of organizations which have substantially improved their overall operational effectiveness, including profitability, once they included "fun" as a goal.

CAN A SENSE OF HUMOR AND PWLOARYK BE DEVELOPED?

It has been said that laughter is God's gift to mankind, but you have to work on your sense of humor. You can consciously apply certain humor principles, and become more competent and joyful, recognizing and taking full advantage of humor opportunities.

This book presents and elaborates upon the principles that Humor Powered people know and use to make their businesses more profitable and to make themselves more attractive, healthier, more successful, content, and joyful. In this book you will find 89 proved ways to have fun at work, along with dozens of solid suggestions for adding humor to everything from bulletin boards to classrooms to your love life.

"When we provide an environment that is pleasant and multidimensional—fun!—we inspire people. They look at things differently. They become more creative and productive." —Fred Pryor

"In general, a spirited environment is marked by laughter—enthusiasm for being on a team and trying darn near anything to make the service or product better." —Tom Peters

"Humor sells. Humor convinces. Humor instructs. Humor entertains. Humor communicates. Humor is the ideal vehicle to capture interest, attention, and approval." —Robert Orben

The power of humor is incredible! It makes you and keeps you satisfied, attractive, creative, productive, healthy, relaxed, optimistic, and profitable. Why aren't more people taking advantage of it?

PERMISSION TO LAUGH

As I have consulted with organizations about putting more humor to work at work, and as I have lectured at training seminars, two important facts have become clear. First, even after people become convinced about the importance of appropriate fun and humor at work, it is still very difficult for some to give themselves permission to loosen up on the job. For many years we have heard the great "shushing" from our parents: "Don't laugh in church;" "Don't laugh at school;" "Don't laugh in the movies." A participant in one of my workshops was often told, "Don't laugh so hard, you'll have a nervous breakdown." Is it any wonder we keep a tight rein on laughter?

Add to this "shushing" a pervasive job ethic, separating work from play, as if combining the two would be sinful. So many of us were

raised with such ideas as, "You can't mix work and play;" "Work is supposed to be hard, not fun;" "Work first, play later," and "Get back to work, we're not here to have fun!" that we envy and distrust people who see their work as fun. Confucius told us to choose occupations that we love so that we might not have to work a day in our lives. We have a serious choice to make.

LACK OF PRACTICE CREATES SKEPTICS

Because of these attitudes, a great many people don't get much practice at mixing work and play. There are few role models to show us how to do it well, and the practice has rarely been rewarded. It is difficult to get people to see how to successfully blend lightness, humor, and fun with work. I am frequently asked by CEOs, managers, and employees:

"How can I be part of the fun at work and still be taken seriously?"

"How can I be humorous if I'm not good at telling jokes?"

"How can I overcome the fact that I just wasn't born with a good sense of humor?"

"Won't having fun hurt our public image?"

"I have a good sense of humor but what can I do about a negative co-worker or boss who doesn't like joking?"

"Doesn't humor take people's minds off of their work?"

"How will we ever get anything accomplished if we're having fun?"

This book is the "how-to" manual that will answer these questions, give you plenty of examples, encourage you to adopt some different attitudes, and reward you for your efforts. (Write to me with your story of how you are having fun at work and helping the job go better, and I will send you an "Official Sense of Humor" certificate that you can frame for all the world to see.)

WHO'S HAVING FUN?

As I meet people of all levels, in all kinds of business organizations, I ask them to tell me about specific ways they are successfully having fun at work. Respondents have included employees of, or consultants to, Armco Steel, Pacific Bell, Hewlett Packard, Ortho Pharmaceutical, Westinghouse, AT&T, Coors Brewing, U. S. Navy, Headstart, Orange & Rockland Utilities, Litton Industries, IBM, University Associates, Digital Equipment, numerous hospitals and universities, and many more. Each idea has been "field tested" somewhere in the United States or Canada and is recommended by the person who used it and found that it worked. In a sense, I have become a clearing-house for ideas that show how organizations make work fun. By sharing these specific examples with you, I hope to inspire you to use them, or create your own ways to implement PWLOARYK, a concept that has proved benefits for employees, customers, and organizations.

COINCIDENCE OR COSMIC ATTRACTION?

As I was finishing this manuscript (The Art of Mixing Work And Play), four events with serious meaning occurred in my life almost simultaneously. In the course of a few days in May, 1991, three reports were published providing the most recent evidence of the effects of stress on productivity, health, and life, and my wife, Pam, and I celebrated a special anniversary.

May 5, 1991, The Akron Beacon Journal: Colin Nickerson of the Boston Globe reports that Japan is beginning to compensate the widows of the 10,000 Japanese executives who die every year from "karoshi," sudden death from overwork. According to the report, Hiroshi Kawahito, a lawyer who heads the Tokyo Office of the National Council for Victims of Karoshi, says, "Japanese are sacrificing their health, and all too often their lives, for the sake of their companies."

Could this happen in the United States? I have seen evidence that it is already happening. According to a prediction by the National Institute of Health, 52% of American executives will die of stress related illnesses. That might not exactly qualify as karoshi, but it is clearly work related. In the last twenty-or-so years, the rate of heart attack among women has increased 100%. This has been attributed primarily to women working in stressful jobs and smoking more. And, there is a report that women are now equal to men in the rate of occurrence of peptic ulcers. Job stress, with its related illnesses and effects on productivity, is sharply on the increase. Readers of this book will learn how the practice of PWLOARYK offers an opportunity to dramatically and positively alter these grim statistics.

On May 7, 1991, USA TODAY: Marilyn Elias reports on the results of research conducted by Dr. Theresa Whiteside, University of Pittsburgh Medical School, showing that stress can wear down immune cells. Among the findings:

-People who have the most aggravation from daily hassles also show the lowest N.K. (Natural Killer) cell activity and experience more illness of all types (N.K. cells are the body's first line of defense against infections and tumors).

-People with low killer cell activity are "more angry and confused" than peers with normal cell function.

-The link between stress, physical immunity, and illness is significant at all ages, but strongest for those under 30. Why would people under 30 get sick more often in the face of daily stress? Dr. Whiteside suggests it is due to lack of perspective.

A well-thought-out PWLOARYK policy at work can provide an organization the perspective and support that can moderate or eliminate many of the effects of stress reported by Dr. Whiteside.

On May 8, 1991, the Associated Press, Minneapolis, reported the findings of a just-released study commissioned by Northwestern National Life Insurance Co. that 34% of American workers seriously considered changing jobs in 1990 because of workplace stress. According to the AP story, Peggy Lawless, Northwestern National's research analyst, said "Job stress and burnout have a foothold in the U. S. workforce without regard to region, size of company, type of job or age of the worker." Among the other findings:

* Seven in ten workers said job stress caused frequent health problems and made them less productive.

* One in three said he expected to burn out on the job by the near future.

* Thirty-four percent said they thought seriously of quitting their jobs last year because of workplace stress. Fourteen percent said workplace stress caused them to quit or change jobs in the last two years.

* Forty-six percent said their jobs are highly stressful, double the percentage cited in the 1985 National Health Interview Survey.

* Fifty-three percent said they were required to work more than 40 hours a week very often or somewhat often.

* Eighty-two percent said victims of burnout deserve disability pay from their employer.

According to the AP report, "The study shows companies with supportive work and family policies, health coverage for mental illness and chemical dependency treatment, improved communication and flex-

An effective policy of PWLOARYK will reduce stress while increasing morale and motivation. *Psychology Today* magazine reviewed several studies of fun and play at work and concluded, "Don't let your dogged determination kill your sense of fun. An element of playfulness will make you more satisfied, more creative and, yes, more productive, too."

May 8, 1991: Pamela And Steve Wilson Celebrate Their 2,700th Anniversary! That is not a science fiction headline. On this day we have been married 2,700 days. You see, we count every day because we want to be reminded to make every day count. Two sudden losses, Pam's first husband to suicide and my mother to ovarian cancer, have made it clear to us that the future is not guaranteed to anyone. We cannot count on having a tenth or fifteenth or twentieth wedding anniversary, so we count and celebrate what we are sure of: today. Those 2,700 daily celebrations have kept our focus on the pleasures and joys that can be found in each day. A sage said, "The past is a cancelled check, you can't spend it anymore. The future is a promissory note which might not be paid off. The present is cash, spend it wisely." Celebrating each day is our way of spending wisely the gift of each day.

I recommend the following practice if you would like to learn to appreciate each day more: Read the obituaries! Two things strike me as I read the obituaries. For one thing, I am fascinated that people die in alphabetical order. But seriously, the obituaries remind us that a lot of people didn't get up this morning. If you are reading this, then you have something to celebrate: you received the gift of life for one more day. Cherish it! Enjoy it!

Is every day a great day for my wife and me? No, but it is one more day we have been given. If we are feeling stressed or pressured (which happens often enough, possibly because we have *four* children in college right now) and we get testy with one another, we remind ourselves of the number of days that we have been married. It is a pleasant anchor to a positive perspective. Happy anniversary, Pam!

A TIME TO LAUGH

Do I think everything is funny? Of course not. It would be naive to think that no matter what happens, you can make a joke about it and then it will be okay. There are tragedies in life. There is a time to laugh and a time to cry. But I believe there are any more opportunities for laughter than most of us take advantage of.

Can we help ourselves by having more fun and feeling positive emotions more often? Absolutely! I think it is our birthright. A rabbi told me that there is an ancient writing which cautions us that when we meet God in the final judgement, we are going to be held accountable for not taking advantage of more of the wonderful things that He put here for us. Imagine that. Our birthright is to enjoy the world into which we are born.

PUZZLE: What is the next item in this series? "Don't Postpone Joy!" "Gather Ye Rosebuds While Ye May," "Carpe Diem," "Eat Desert First" . . .

ANSWER: PWLOARYK.

Mixing work and play can help you love your job and prevent stress, burnout and karoshi, keep you sane and healthy, and make you a better lover. I urge you to try it.

In the next chapter, you will learn what to do if, like many people, you wonder about your sense of humor, or wonder about your ability to mix work and play, because you cannot tell jokes. From there, you will be introduced to specific guidelines--The PWLOARYK Principles--for ensuring that when you mix work and play you get positive results. You will find specific ways people are mixing work and play in organizations throughout the United States and Canada. Then you will read about the wise "whys" and "hows" of mixing work and play to foster higher quality in businesses, classrooms, and your love life. The final chapters are direct, instrumental support for your efforts--a calendar of more than 100 unusual-but-true reasons to celebrate, and humorous posters for faxing or to brighten up the company bulletin board.

If you can't quit your job, move to the country, start your own business, or otherwise downshift, why not make your job more fun by mixing work and play? Humor, laughter, and play are in your future. Read on.

CHAPTER 2

KEEP YOUR FUNNY SIDE UP: DISCOVER THE HUMOR PERSPECTIVE

Here's a sobering prediction I came across not too long ago: fifty-two percent of American executives will die of stress-related illnesses. As a psychologist, I know that a good deal of the emotional tension and stress experienced by those executives will not be caused by the events in their lives. Rather, the stress will be caused by their *perceptions* of those events. It is not what is happening to us that hurts us so much as what we *think about* what is happening to us.

GOOD NEWS/BAD NEWS

How would you react if you received notice that the Post Office was trying to deliver an unexpected certified letter to you? If you thought it was bad news, you might react with trembling, with butterflies or knots in your stomach, increased heart-rate and blood pressure, and/or perspiration--in other words, with worry and stress. But if you imagine that the letter would tell you that you have inherited a fortune and that all your troubles are over, you'd probably have no knots, no trembling, no skyrocketing blood pressure, no worry, no stress. You might even giggle. It all depends on what you *think* is going to happen. If you look at all sides of a situation, you will eventually find a side that you think is absurd, ludicrous, zany, or ironic. Find the laughable side of a situation and you will reduce the emotional tension that is part of stress.

Humor provides an emotional distancing. Your perspective changes when you step back and take a second (or third) look at things. Troubles don't seem as large, and you can see more of the resources that you have available to help you solve your problem. Alan Cohen encourages us, commenting that "Laughter lifts us over high ridges and lights up dark valleys in a way that makes life so much better."

There is always another way to look at things. There is more than one way to skin a cat. Life is a balance of opposites. Yin and Yang; the Ecclesiastical "time for all things": planting and harvesting, coming and going, crying and laughing. When you look at the proverbial glass of water, do you see one that is half full or one that is half empty? Personally, I see a glass that is twice as large as it needs to be (which is yet another way of looking at it)!

An excellent way to handle emotional tension or stress, especially the minor irritations, is to look not just at both sides, but at all sides of the situation. And look for the humorous side while you're at it.

GRACE UNDER PRESSURE

You help yourself by having that A-Number-One all-important special sense of humor: the ability to laugh at yourself. According to psychologist Harvey Mindess, Ph.D., "Though we make fun of ourselves for being stupid or lazy or klutzy, by laughing at those flaws, what we are really saying is we're lovable nonetheless." Develop your sense of humor and you will find it easier to see all sides of a situation.

Can you do it? Can you see your own shortcomings as funny foibles rather than fearsome failings? Can you take yourself lightly when the crunch comes? If so, you will certainly handle problems better, keeping your blood pressure at healthier levels. And there are bonuses such as winning the admiration of your co-workers for your ability to quell panic, get the job done, and not be disturbed by disappointment or discouragement. Lily Tomlin wryly observed, "The trouble with the rat race is that even if you win you're still a rat!"

Cultivate the ability to see the lighter side to everyday life and you won't feel defeated nearly as often. Take the joke on yourself in a good-natured way and it will be impossible for others to make jokes about you. If you don't feel very creative in this regard, just look around for examples from others who are able to adopt this attitude. Try to learn from them, but at least, borrow from them. I know of a secretary who, when she drops the telephone (who hasn't?), retrieves it and tells the caller, "Oh, you must be on candid telephone today." She doesn't get flustered or embarrassed or make excuses. She stays in control of the situation, maintains her poise and dignity, and gets the job done, probably winning the respect of the caller, too.

WHO ARE YOU LAUGHING AT?

You might try your hand at making up fun descriptions as one way of coping with the tougher parts of your work. Here is a job definition which might help teachers have a good laugh at themselves: "A teacher is a person who can drink three cups of coffee before eight o'clock in the morning and hold them till three o'clock in the afternoon!" (Of course, teachers have a lot of class!) One nurse says that sometimes she thinks R.N. stands for "Real Nut." (And we all know that nurses call the shots!)

Shakespeare created a play on words which compares a shoemaker to a clergyman: "A cobbler is a mender of men's soles (souls)." Radio commentator Paul Harvey has fun with bumper stickers, which he calls "bumper snickers." Many of them are job-related: "Plumbers go with the flow!" "Electricians want your shorts!" "Bakers roll in the dough!" And, "Doctors need a lot of patients!" What is your job like? Can you think of a phrase that will put it into a humorous and healthier perspective? We have choices about how we look at the things that happen to us. Reader's Digest compiled some questions which show that common annoyances can seem less irritating once you find an uncommon way of looking at them. Here are a few examples:

"Where else but in Washington, D.C. would they call the department that's in charge of everything outdoors the Department of the Interior?"

"Why is it called baby-sitting when all you do is run after them?"

"Why are income taxes due April 15, the same day the Titanic went down?"

"How come the windshield wiper always works better on the passenger side?"

And the Los Angeles Times Syndicate poses this metaphorical question: "Do you ever feel that life is a car wash and you're going through it on a bicycle?"

My sense of humor? I realize that not everything is funny and that laughter can be completely out of place if the timing is wrong. But the next time life's little foul-ups are getting to me, I'm going to see if I can find the comic's perspective and use my wittiness to outwit the dimwits and the nitwits and . . . *RELAX*. You can do it, too!

CHAPTER 3

THE PWLOARYK PRINCIPLES

The principles presented in this chapter are widely accepted and easy to understand. The idea is to give you and your fellow employees a set of guidelines that make sense and are easy to apply, too. They are based on published research, field observation, and common sense. Here are the Do's and Don'ts you need for successful PWLOARYK.

HOW MANY EXECUTIVES DOES IT TAKE TO CHANGE A LIGHT BULB?

What makes something funny? What constitutes "fun"? Be careful who you ask. Almost everyone under the sun has a theory about what makes an activity fun or a joke funny. Sociologist John Bowman suggests that fun is a very subjective and personal thing, meaning that what I like to do for fun might not appeal to you, and vice versa. Fun is a matter of taste, and tastes vary—which is just as well, because this gives a rich variety in everything from hobbies to humorists to ways of having fun at work.

Many of the attempts at scientific explanations of humor are dry at best, and incomprehensibly confusing at worst. Linguist Victor Raskin begins his explanation of jokes with: "The semantic theory of humor uses a formal, script-based lexicon and combinatorial rules to match the informal, intuitive analysis listeners make when they hear a joke." You could get a headache trying to follow this reasoning.

Here is a joke which has been analyzed in an attempt to figure out what's funny and why: "Is the doctor in?" the patient asked in his bronchial whisper. "No," the doctor's young and pretty wife whispered in reply. "Come right in." Raskin's technical analysis of just this one joke takes 10 pages in his book *Semantic Mechanisms of Humor*. I won't be so painstaking in giving you the psychologically correct low-down on how to mix work and play.

Before you actually get started, and all along the way, it will be helpful to review some of the basic principles of human nature, as well as the scientific evidence that PWLOARYK really works. Thus grounded in theory, you will know what to expect and why. This summary of facts and observations lays the foundation for forming new attitudes and trying new behaviors which will lead to achievements and satisfactions that you may never have thought possible.

PRINCIPLE I: "FUN" is a subjective term.

Fun means different things to different people. Sociologist John Bowman, Ph.D., reminds us that many workers still operate under the misconception, derived from the 500 year old puritan Protestant ethic, that work is to be exalted while amusement is forbidden. There is a growing body of research which proves that work and fun, or work and play, are not opposites, and when they are blended together appropriately, everybody benefits.

Jim Pelley, Director of Everything at Laughter Works Seminars, Sacramento, California, recommends that you become a CEO/HOHO (Creative Employee Organizer Who Helps Others Handle Obstacles). He cites numerous examples of companies engaging in MBHA: Management by Horsing Around, with highly desirable results.

PRINCIPLE II: **Work cannot always be play, but work can often be fun.**

As you will learn from ideas collected from successful work groups, fun can mean brainstorming, celebration, festivity, frivolity, pitching-in, being supportive, giving rewards and recognition, playing games, learning, laughing, joking, or relaxing together. Physiologically and psychologically, "fun" is actually a metaphor for all of the positive emotions.

"Fun" at work may be defined as any positive interaction that enhances the employees' psychological or physiological well-being. From that point of view it is easy to see how one's productive capabilities, as well as a host of other elements of job performance, are enhanced.

PRINCIPLE III: **While you are developing your sense of humor, it is a good idea to develop your sensitivity to humor.**

An old maxim of comedy holds that "timing is everything." This holds true for using humor on the job. Humor is not appropriate to every situation. PWLOARYK is not a matter of any humor at any time; it is a matter of the right humor at the right time. Knowing the difference can make quite a difference.

Julie Mitchell, Communications Manager for Adia Personnel Services, Menlo Park, California, passed along to me the results of one of the few surveys conducted to find out what people think about humor at work. In one part of the survey, 1,160 human resource professionals were asked for their opinions as to when humor is appropriate. Their answers indicated that they thought humor is appropriate in a variety of job situations, but not all the time. The percentage who said humor was okay in each of the following situations was as follows:

- when discussing a problem with a colleague (72%);
- during a job interview (63%);
- during a performance interview (58%);
- during a tense moment in a meeting (53%);
- with a direct supervisor (46%);
- when meeting the top brass (40%);
- when dealing with a client complaint or problem (21%).

How would your answers compare to the survey findings? Check with some of your co-workers and those one level above and one level below your position. This is a way to start to get a sense of the humor climate on your job. It is important for you to understand how those around you look at humor on the job because going against the grain of humor sensibilities can have unpleasant effects.

PRINCIPLE IV: The key to preventing physical and emotional burn-out is balance.

James Loehr, Ph.D., a sports psychologist who studies "ideal performance state," has found that the balanced diet for stamina and stress resistance is obtained by getting 60% of your calories from carbohydrates, 25% of your calories from fats, and 15% of your calories from protein. He also notes that athletes who perform superbly in the "ideal performance state" experience high energy, excitement, and fun, and they have a good balance in their work/rest cycles.

But these balances will not be enough to ward off the ill-effects of stress which, if unabated, ends in physical and emotional burnout. The key element which must be balanced is perspective. Most stress is not the result of what is happening to us as much as it is a result of how we perceive what is happening to us. One of the best descriptions of the psychological dynamics of stress is that it is the result of two appraisals we make (perhaps unconsciously). We appraise the situation as to what we think is at stake, and we appraise our resources for dealing with the situation. When we believe that the situation will overtax our resources, we go into the kind of stress that eventually can make us sick.

Many people over-estimate the importance of situations. This is called making mountains out of molehills. (It is not a coincidence that terms like "dying of embarrassment," "worried sick," and "pressing deadlines" have serious implications. Personally, I think dying of embarrassment is pretty extreme, and I try to avoid the word "deadline"). At the same time, there seems to be an epidemic of low self-esteem going around which means that many people underestimate their capabilities for handling situations. When you overestimate what's at stake and underestimate your resources, your brain chemistry and total physiology change, suppressing your immune functions, among other things, and you are right on target for a severe stress reaction.

One of the most natural ways to keep a balanced perspective is to have a good sense of humor. Humor is a way of seeing things in another perspective, as if from a distance, so you see things in more nearly their correct proportions. From that perspective you are less likely to feel overwhelmed, and more likely to feel sane and to stay healthy.

EXAMPLE: A photograph in a newspaper showed a man standing next to his car, which had been crushed by a tree during a storm. He was facing the passing traffic, holding up a sign which had an arrow on it pointing to his car. The sign said, "Compact Car." Now, the man surely knew that the humorous sign would fix neither the tree nor his car. But, in a situation like that, one often has the option of cracking up with stress or cracking up with laughter. The laughter provides physical and emotional protection, leaving one better able to deal with insurance companies, mechanics, missed appointments, and the like.

Making the choice of humor in a situation such as the above is the result of first having made an "R.M.A: Rapid Mental Adjustment." You can learn to make RMAs in any number of situations in which there doesn't seem to be anything else you can do. Practice making RMAs and you will find yourself becoming a more accepting and relaxed person.

Take the process of aging, for example. As much as we might be a youth-oriented society, everybody is aging and, if you are lucky, you might even live eighty or ninety years or more. George Burns says, "You can't help growing older, but you can help getting old; that is a state of mind." You can be 36 years old or 70 years young. Whether or not you get stressed out over things, especially those which are essentially beyond your control, depends on how you look at them. In this regard, RMAs and a good sense of humor are lifesavers.

PRINCIPLE V: A good sense of humor means being able to see the absurd, ludicrous, or laughable side of a situation—it does not have to mean telling jokes.

You can display a wonderful sense of humor and get all of the benefits of fun at work without ever having to tell a joke. In fact, you may know some people who can tell jokes fairly well, but they can't see the humor in something that isn't going the way it should right now. They don't have a very well-developed sense of humor.

Being able to tell jokes is not always advisable, either. Charles J. Givens, a self-made expert on creating and maintaining wealth, author of the best-selling *Wealth Without Risks,* has some interesting words of caution along this line. A report of Givens' philosophy, methods, and success was documented in *Personal Selling Power for Sales Success* (July/August 1991). Especially for those who want to be successful in sales, he points out the importance of being true to your self ("If I sit down with a prospect," he says, "and tell him all my jokes, that's not part of me"). Givens makes a distinction between telling stories and telling jokes. "Salespeople tell jokes because of the experience of acceptance. The salesman sits down at the bar and everybody laughs when he tells a joke. It's easy to transfer that into thinking that if you do that in a sales situation, it's going to put people at ease and make them feel comfortable with you. That's not true at all (I disagree - S.W.). But a good story is personal. I'm sharing something and, as long as the story is appropriate for the situation, people love to listen."

So you may be terrible at telling jokes and still have a terrific sense of humor, if you can see the funny side of a situation you have been a part of, if you can laugh about it even when it exposes your own foibles, and if you can relate that funny episode to others. A well-developed sense of humor is not so much a matter of *being* funny, it is much more a matter of *seeing* funny. I have found that approximately 90% of people feel they have a good sense of humor. And, oddly, at least two studies show that 89% of folks rate themselves as "above average" in sense of humor. (I find it humorous that it is statistically impossible for 89% of people to be above average.) However, among the same group there is agreement that only about 5% feel that they can tell a joke really well. This means that the 75% of companies in the Adia survey that encourage joke telling to break the ice at staff meetings are asking for the impossible (or they are getting a lot of very badly told jokes). It would be far more productive to break the ice at meetings by asking those in attendance to bring and pass around a cartoon which they find funny.

Is it hard to get people to loosen up and do some positive joking with each other? "Perhaps the most secret thing about executive jocularity," says Walter Kiechel III, in a 1983 *FORBES* article, "is how easy it is to achieve: if you indicate the slightest willingness to laugh, jokes will walk right up to you, delivered by subordinates, peers, maybe the boss. Look for humor, expect it. Soon you'll probably see its laughing face everywhere, even smirking from behind the solemn, workaday visages of your fellow managers."

PRINCIPLE VI: When we are in humor, or any positive emotion, our brain chemistry changes.

In turn, our physiology changes in ways that help us resist illness, avert the effects of stress, and stay healthy. Some of the physiological changes known to accompany humor and other positive emotions are:

- production of endorphins, the body's natural painkillers;
- increased respiration, exercising the lungs, diaphragm, and various parts of the musculo-skeletal system;
- increased uptake and distribution of oxygen to all parts of the body, including the brain;

- activation of the limbic system, a part of the central nervous system, which helps insure "whole brain" thinking;

- a cardiovascular workout, with increases in heart rate and blood pressure, followed by normalization of blood pressure;

- a euphoriant effect of pleasant emotions;

- muscular relaxation (muscular tension is part of emotional tension, which is part of the stress reactions);

- activation of the immune system to produce natural killer cells, the body's first line of defense against invading organisms.

These effects account for the contention that you don't laugh because you feel good, you feel good because you laugh! So, happy employees are healthy employees, and they are on the job rather than at home or out fishing or playing golf taking "sick leave." (Did you know that half of the people who call in sick actually are? The rest just don't want to waste a perfectly good sick day on illness.)

One fellow called in to work and reported to his supervisor, "I've been sick ever since I came to work for you. I'm feeling good today, so I'm not coming in!"

PRINCIPLE VII: Mixing work and play will be counterproductive when employees are immature, angry, or poorly trained in the value of fun.

Supervisors would be well-advised to take the necessary steps to correct any of these conditions should they occur. The Adia survey asked human resource professionals what method not currently in effect would boost morale. The overwhelming answer was "hire a humor consultant."

PRINCIPLE VIII: When managers deny employees the opportunity for harmless mixing of work and play, the employees will be resentful and engage in covert play (or sabotage).

Most employees are well aware of whether or not their actions are interfering with production. It they are not hurting production with their fun or humor, they will feel as if they are being treated like children when the supervisor tells them to stop. This is not going to be very well received, to say the least.

A number of experts in the area of the psychology of job performance, including Charles Garfield, Ph.D., author of the best-selling book *Peak Performance,* have observed some pretty consistent motivations for playfulness. They have concluded that when the work is highly demanding, highly responsible, boring, or repetitive there is a natural inclination on the part of workers to seek out balance through fun and humor. Dr. Garfield says that he observes humor to be one of the elements present in all groups and individuals achieving peak performance.

So if the boss doesn't allow appropriate humor and fun "breaks," the employees will wait until the boss is away and then break out the party hats and boogie. Resentful employees, laughing at such supervisors behind their backs, sabotage projects, don't work as hard as they could, and withhold their best ideas.

PRINCIPLE IX: All aspects of mixing work and play must be positive.

Anyone who has had their spirits lifted by humor knows that humor is an important tool. On the other hand, anyone who has been the butt of a joke, or who has been part of a group that has been made fun of, knows that humor can be a destructive weapon, too. Humor can help and humor can hurt. Humor can lift people up or slam them down. Humor that offends people turns them off. When that happens, you can't teach them anything, sell them anything, or motivate them to do anything. Racial jokes, ethnic slurs, sexist humor, put-down zingers, embarrassment, sarcasm, and ridicule all should be eliminated. The richest laugh comes at no one's expense.

Here are the Humor Golden Rules, the most effective guidelines for keeping humor powerfully positive:

1. Always be aware of your audience and your position. Humor that is incongruent with your position may be confusing and may reduce your credibility. The humor that works well with your close friends may not be acceptable to your customers; the "inside" jokes of your work group may not go over well with your family.

2. Think about the person or the group you are about to engage in humor or play. Knowing them as you do, ask yourself if the humor will, from their perspective, be appropriate and tasteful.

3. Consider the timing. Humor is not always welcome, at least not right away. It may be too soon after a hurt to try to elicit a positive response to humor. When a person is recuperating from an appendectomy and has fresh stitches, it is probably not the best time to try to get them to laugh.

4. Eliminate sarcasm and ridicule. Sarcasm is the most easily misinterpreted of all forms of communication because you are conveying what you mean by saying exactly what you do not mean. Ridicule is unacceptable for obvious reasons.

5. Erase taboo language. The sense of which language is acceptable will vary from group to group. Give it strong consideration.

6. Be very careful when making humorous comments about a serious subject; it gives a mixed message and may be taken the wrong way.

7. Be careful of where you use gratuitous humor (telling a joke for the sake of the joke). With customers, trainees, or when making a presentation, use humor that serves to illustrate points or connect you to others.

8. Invoke "The Five Minute Rule": Don't poke fun at anything another person could not change in the next five minutes. And even then, be sensitive!

9. Whenever possible, make fun of situations rather than making fun of people.

10. Take the joke on yourself. Always do this in a way that shows you have self-acceptance. Never put yourself down or demean yourself with humor. Be kind to others and to yourself, too.

There is an African proverb that sums this up: "The axe forgets, but the tree remembers."

PRINCIPLE X: Learn to appreciate the difference between being "stupid" and being "silly."

There is no value for you in being stupid, so don't be stupid, and don't try to make others look stupid. However, sometimes, silliness is the wisest alternative, and you would do well to act silly and to invite others to do the same. But do not do things to "make" others look silly, unless you are absolutely certain it is okay with them.

If you are too worried about being cool to look silly, remember that the word silly itself comes from the Old English word "saelig," meaning "happy, prosperous, and blessed."

PRINCIPLE XI: Humor works best to moderate minor irritations and help people to get along better.

The really big problems are not likely to be a laughing matter, at least not right away. You probably do not know anyone who has been mauled by a lion or trampled by an elephant. But I'll bet you do know many people who have been bitten by mosquitos or stung by bees. MORAL: It's the little things that get you! So use humor mostly to deal with the little things that go wrong. Stay in balance about the dozens of minor problems which are sure to crop up each day, and you and your team will be stronger and more resilient when it comes to handling the big ones. There may be some humor in a big problem, but even if there isn't, you will have more stamina for dealing with the big ones if you have been using humor all along to deal with the little ones.

In the December 12, 1983 *FORBES*, Walter Kiechel III said that every manager's bag of tricks should include a sense of humor. He quotes William Gould, Executive Vice President of the Association of Executive Search Consultants, explaining why he would never offer a client a humorless candidate: "What companies are seeking is someone who can see issues clearly. If a person can laugh, particularly at himself, he can probably step back and get the right perspective on things."

Kiechel sees the values of the managerial use of humor as diffusing tense situations, creating rapport, creating perceptions of power, making difficult messages more agreeable, avoiding potentially sticky situations, letting the troops know how you are concerned about something without hammering on it, and building team cohesion. Pretty powerful results. And not too hard to come by when you follow these principles.

PRINCIPLE XII: Take "humor breaks." Punctuate the work day with opportunities for mixing work and play.

In the Adia survey, 39% of personnel directors felt that laugh breaks are more desirable than coffee breaks. You can benefit from as little as five minutes a day of fun and humor, if you do it one minute at a time. Figure out ways to lighten up for one minute at a time and use your "humor breaks" as shock absorbers to take up the jolts of mistakes and other frustrations. Henry Ward Beecher said, "A person without a sense of humor is like a wagon without springs: jolted by every pebble in the road."

If you go through all the stresses and strains of the workday without some humor breaks, you will not get much benefit from going home and trying to relax by taking a hot bath or watching a sitcom on TV. That is like putting the shock absorbers on your car after the trip is over! You need them all along the way. Build several PWLOARYK breaks into each day at work.

PRINCIPLE XIII: Mixing work and play is voluntary, something you do because you want to, not because you have to.

The concept of play has many meanings and may be misunderstood from time to time. We "play" light-hearted games to invite giggles (peek-a-boo with infants), but we also use the word "play" for sports like football, which can be very serious and dangerous business. Play can either mean a cooperative activity or a competitive activity, and there is a world of difference between the two. In recent years, those who study these things have begun to question the traditionally heralded value of competition. Perhaps, some suggest, for many purposes it is best to compete only against one's own record. In business, they say, one should aim for cooperation between departments within a company but compete against other companies, not against parts of your own organization. Some experts urge us to promote "win-win" outcomes both in-house and as the result of all negotiations.

In my private practice, I have treated more than one stressed-out executive who was goal-driven and out to win in every part of life. They achieved a good measure of relief when, among other things, they learned to understand the distinction between play and playfulness. Some of the high-powered, hard-driven individuals are intensely competitive. They carry their competitiveness home from the office, into all aspects of their social and recreational lives, to the annoyance and chagrin of their families and friends.

These win-at-all-costs types cannot enjoy a friendly game of golf, tennis, cards, Monopoly, Trivial Pursuit, or Chutes 'n Ladders. This loss of balance, loss of ability to enjoy playfulness, is destructive to one's health and to one's most important relationships.

I know people who set out to relax by playing golf or tennis, but they allow scoring and winning to become the priority, so they end up more tense than they were before they went out to play. My advice to anyone who falls into this pattern is to practice playfulness from time to time. To help you understand exactly what that means, take a look at these characteristics of "true play."

CHARACTERISTICS OF PLAY: DIFFERENTIATING PLAY FROM OTHER ACTIVITIES

1. ***Play is not relaxation.*** Play is quite different from relaxation. During relaxation response a person's total body system slows down; heart rate and blood pressure decrease. Relaxation is an integrated central and autonomic nervous system response in which one reduces both mental and physical activity to a minimum. Play, on the other hand, is spontaneous, joyful, expressive, and often very active. Blood pressure and heart rate actually increase (and subsequently decrease) with joyful laughter and play. There's improved circulation and cardiac efficiency, related to increased oxygenation which takes place, which is similar to that provided by aerobic exercise.

2. ***Play May Be Exercise, But It Need Not Be.*** Exercise and play are often confused. One may exercise in a playful way, such as when a

humorous attitude is adopted while playing tennis. Play may also involve an exercise activity such as playing a game of *Frisbee* with a group of friends. All exercise is not play, however, and all play is not exercise. People at times have difficulty differentiating these two activities. One person, for example, reported that he jogged 15 minutes that day and thought that jogging was a play activity. With further questioning, though, he stated that he perceived jogging as a "boring struggle" which he practiced because he knew it was good for his heart. Jogging was clearly not a playful activity for this person. Each person's attitude toward an activity has a major role in differentiating play from other activities.

3. ***Competition is Not a Major Component of Play.*** Competition is not a primary motive of good play. While a person may enjoy winning a tennis game with a friend in healthy play, winning is not a prerequisite for having fun. The concept of doing something "just for fun" is foreign to most competitive, time-driven people. A constant need to win (for example, to have the best running time or the best score at racquetball) is often in conflict with their intellectual knowledge of the value of playing just for fun. Healthy play can provide situations in which everybody wins and no one loses.

4. ***Play May Be Passive and/or Active.*** Good play leaves one feeling refreshed, happy, and alive. It is frequently a spontaneous activity that provides release, exhilaration, and refreshment. This is quite different from the passive experience of watching television. Most people could not say that they feel good, happy, or alive after watching four hours of television. Although play is often active, it can be passive and still leave the person feeling exhilarated and refreshed. Fun stops when one has to play, a common occurrence when school children are encouraged to go outside and "play" (for example, soccer or jump rope). In our example, 10 year old Colin said, "No, I want to sit here on the windowsill and write a poem." This, too, would leave Colin feeling refreshed, happy, and alive; this is true play.

5. ***Work For One Person May Be Play For Another Person.*** It is important to pay attention to the fact that the perception of an activity as playful is unique to the individual. Some people hate working in their yards, pulling weeds, and mowing grass.

For others, this is an extremely playful activity and one that they look forward to all week. Appreciation of these unique perceptions is vital. If a person considers something playful, he or she must understand that another person may have a very different perception of that activity.

6. ***Play is a Preoccupied State.*** When engaging in true, healthy play, a person becomes preoccupied and totally immersed in the pleasurable experience. Most adults are aware of children's inability to hear Dad calling them to dinner while they are engrossed in play. For adults, it is more difficult and unusual for this state to be reached, although sexual play provides one example. Adults also occasionally become preoccupied during social play (playing cards or watching a stage play) and are able to "lose themselves" in the pleasurable experience.

7. ***Play is Noncumulative.*** A common misconception is that fun time or playful times are only for weekends or yearly vacations. Some people will intellectually understand that these types of playful times are vital for health but will participate in them only for brief, isolated periods each week or each month. To be most effective in maintaining health and preventing or managing illness, play, like all other self-care activities, must be practiced regularly.

People cannot "save up" all of their play activities for a yearly vacation and expect to obtain effective, long-term perspective.

8. ***Play Usually Involves Humor and Spontaneous Laughter.*** Play is always the opposite of seriousness, even though it may occur during serious times. A sense of freedom and stimulation is associated with the experience of a good laugh. The ability to laugh at oneself places stressful problems in a new perspective.

9. ***Play Involves Freedom of Choice.*** The experience of not being constrained by others or by circumstances is a major component of play. This, again, is a difficult and confusing area for many people. A person reported that she went bicycling with her children. The major motive in this activity, however, was to allay the guilt she felt in having so little time for play with them. In this circumstance, the person was probably constrained by others (children) and was not experiencing the bicycling simply for her own pleasure.

When you engage in activities that have these nine characteristics you will be more relaxed, and you will be practicing some of the attitudes necessary for successful PWLOARYK.

EXERCISE: See how many competitive games you can change to cooperative win-win activities by making a few changes in the rules or in the ultimate objectives. Virtually any activity, game, or sport that is usually played competitively can, with some modification of the rules, be played cooperatively. For example, the competitive objective in a standard game of volleyball is to make the other team "miss" or be unable to return the ball over the net. By changing the objective to "seeing how long we can keep up the volley," the teams cooperate and, as the overall score improves—the volley gets longer—everybody wins.

***Adapted from S. Baldi, et al, reported in *For Your Health: A Model for Self-Care* (South Laguna, Ca.: Nurses Model health, 1980), p. 119, and L. Hill and N. Smith, *Self-Care Nursing*, Appleton-Century-Crofts, 1983.**

PRINCIPLE XIV: Issue invitations for others to join in the fun, don't demand that they participate.

Beware of the person who says, "I'm going to make you laugh." This statement implies a form of force or control. In fact, we do best when we decide for ourselves how we would like to respond to situations. I have sometimes heard parents, when they are upset with their crying children, say "I'll give you something to cry about" or, "I'll make you really cry." We do not need anyone to make us cry or make us laugh in the sense that they may be trying to control us.

Being cheered up when one is not ready to be cheered up can be dreadful. Allow others to "pass" when they are not in the mood. Do not become overbearing by insisting that everyone have a good time at the same time.

PRINCIPLE XV: Create opportunities for mixing work and play which take into account individual tastes and needs.

Some folks enjoy bowling and others would rather decorate for a party. Some just want to see a cartoon on the bulletin board.

The Adia survey found that 75% of employers encourage workers to display humorous cards and comic strips in their private work spaces. This is fine, but it doesn't go far enough. It does help, when things are getting tense, to be able to spot the funny poster or sign you hung at your work area. But did you know that if you put a few cartoons on a bulletin board, more employees will stay longer to read more of the other messages put there? And if you set aside even a corner of the bulletin board for the "Joke Or Cartoon Of The Week," more people will come around more often to get the new humor and read the new messages. A great way to improve communications!

PRINCIPLE XVI: Organize a group to help get the fun going and ask for suggestions.

Try forming a volunteer *PWLOARYK Committee* or *Fun Committee* whose responsibility is to come up with ways to provide your workplace with a balance of fun and playfulness, for a month at a time. Steve Allen, Jr. recommends that companies choose a person who would be relieved of regular job duties for a day and would be required to infuse humor into the workplace. He suggests calling this person "*The Company Tickler.*"

For a large organization, form committees in each department or work area, as well as for larger units. Try a rotating membership, so everyone gets a turn, and no one has to do it all the time.

Use a survey or suggestion box to get input from as many employees as possible. Encourage them to drop in their nominations for the

"Joke or Cartoon of the Week." Sorting through the suggestions or complaints will then become a little more fun.

PRINCIPLE XVII: Don't worry about the sourpusses.

Pay little heed to those who say "We're not here to have fun." Many supervisors are afraid to lighten up because they think the employees won't take them seriously. They may suffer from anhedonia, the inability to experience guilt-free pleasure, a condition which, according to Dr. Harold Bloomfield, afflicts many people these days. These people are "humor impaired," and they need help. You probably know some folks at work who are "humor impaired." They are that way for reasons that make sense to them. You cannot make them change, but you can show them that you can create a safe, non-embarrassing, productive environment for fun, and let them know they are invited to join in anytime they want to. Sooner or later, many of them will come around.

PRINCIPLE XVIII: You don't have to stop being serious to be humorous or to mix work and play.

This sounds like a paradox until you realize that when you get into humor, what you actually give up is solemnity. People who are overly solemn tend to take themselves too seriously (and because of the ill-effects of stress, they may become "terminally serious"). They may be pompous (suffering from "occupational dignity"), or preoccupied with their position ("title-itis").

You can remain serious about your responsibilities, serious about your values, serious about your beliefs, and serious about your goals, and still take yourself and a situation lightly when it is appropriate. Susan Goodman, in a 1989 *CURRENT HEALTH*, reports "Studies have shown that a sense of humor is the most consistent characteristic among executives promoted in major companies. Scientists have found that if you smile, you are more likely to be hired for a job. You are also more likely to be trusted once in that job." According to William Fry, Jr., M.D., in all the recorded history of medicine no one has ever died laughing, but the term "dead serious" is one we had better listen to.

FUNNYBONE: In one office I visited, the manager was quite taken with himself and walked around pointing out to the employees, "I'm the boss, you're nothing!" Several times a day he could be heard gloating, "I'm the boss, you're nothing. I'm the boss, you're nothing." This obnoxious practice came to a halt the day a secretary, having had her fill of his pomposity, stood up and retorted in full earshot of the entire office, "That's a big deal . .„. boss over nothing!"

PRINCIPLE XIX: Lighten up.

We live in a society that places a high value on self-control and takes that value to an unhealthy extreme with admonishments to "control yourself." Teachers, parents, supervisors, and others in authority often believe that "to grow up you must grim up" and they echo sentiments such as "Would you please control yourself?" and "Could you just control yourself" as a way of trying to shut off laughter. In the "All In The Family" television series, Norman Lear showed that the admonition to "Stifle it!" is reflective of the *Archie Bunker* mentality. Repressive.

It is no wonder that we experience anhedonic and humor impaired people as negative. They can't seem to stand to see anyone having a good time. Mixing work and play is a way for you to nurture the spontaneous, fun-loving, joyful parts of yourself and others.

PRINCIPLE XX: There is a time to laugh and time to cry.

Laughing and crying serve the very necessary function of providing natural emotional release from tension (which is often part of stress). When you tell a person to stop laughing (or crying) you are interrupting an important outlet. Bottling up emotions, in turn, causes all sorts of problems down the road. Then, sometime later, they come to see me or my therapist colleagues and pay a great deal of money for help in getting the cork out of the bottle and getting their emotions and perspectives straightened out. It is much better to laugh (or cry) as the situation warrants and stay healthy all along.

PRINCIPLE XXI: "Funny" is in the eye of the be-ho-ho-holder.

Whenever you are enjoying humor with other people, there is an interaction among three elements which deserves careful consideration. The three elements are the audience (even if it is only one other person), the material, and the situation. For example, the type of humor that for ten years was shared at the beginning of each session of my Men's Support Group would not be appropriate with the United Methodist Academy of Clergy or Mary Kay Cosmetics beauty consultants (I have presented humor workshops for both groups).

Poking fun at very serious situations has its dangers, too. Making jokes about the nuclear accident at Chernobyl may confuse young children: is it O.K. to laugh at them because it didn't happen to us? For a short time after the United States began military efforts to remove Saddam Hussein from Kuwait, there seemed to be a moratorium on jokes about the war. After a few weeks, the jokes started. At first, humorists were tentative with their humor about the Gulf War, testing the waters of the audiences' sensitivities. The longer the war continued, however, the more we needed humor, and it came out in earnest, increasing in quantity and strength.

SOME PERSONAL EXAMPLES

(1) A long-standing rule of comedy says, "Timing is everything." Here is one personal example (there have been others) of bad timing: funny material, but at the wrong time.

At the age of 14, my son Shawn was hospitalized for an emergency appendectomy. As soon as the surgeon pronounced the operation a success, I was prepared to invoke humor to help with his healing. The day after his surgery, I arrived at Children's Hospital in Dayton, Ohio, went directly to his bedside, and started in with the jokes and antics I knew would make him laugh. This was not a good idea.

He tried to go along with me but after 30 seconds I saw that he had tears in his eyes as he begged me, "No more, Dad, please! I have stitches and the laughing is killing me!" I felt terrible at the time, that I might have done anything to hurt him. Now we can look back on that incident and laugh. As Mark Twain put it, "Humor is tragedy, plus time."

(2) Another personal example (I told you there were more). Early in my career as a professional speaker I made a couple of mistakes which have probably cost me some business and left some people with the wrong impression about me.

In my earlier days of professional speaking I was not very skilled at sizing up the sensitivities of my audience and I was letting my ego (rather than the needs of the audience) dictate the selection of my material. I wanted to teach audiences not to be so uptight about certain subjects. I was eager to impress them with my ability to deal comfortably with sensitive subject matter. My material has never been "blue" or the locker-room variety, but it was colorful enough to be offensive to some people, and I stepped on some toes.

When we all first became aware that AIDS was a national problem, I thought it would be a good idea to talk about it and, at the same time, illustrate some of the powers of humor. I worked up a funny piece of material which used humorous condoms as "props" (some were available commercially and some were custom-made locally in Columbus, Ohio by a company called "Condom Creations by Jane" whose motto was "For Our Country's Preservation We Must Become a Condom Nation").

I still believe the "bit" demonstrated how humor could help us deal with situations that make us uncomfortable, overcome resistance to using prophylactics, and help to fight a horrible scourge. But I liked the material so much that I started using it with every group to which I spoke. The effectiveness of the illustration was lost on some of the more conservative groups, and my credibility with them was soon shot. But other groups—medical, health care, university educators—loved it! I quickly learned the necessity and value of thinking of others and putting their needs ahead of my own.

I can't be sure of exactly who was offended, so I offer my apology now to all those who got more than they bargained for. Now that I have become more Humor Powered and learned that the audience comes first, I have redeemed myself many times over.

HUMOR POWER POINTERS:

1. The audience's needs and sensitivities are more important than your own.
2. Timing is everything.
3. What is funny in one situation may not be funny in another situation.

HUMOR POWER QUOTATIONS:

"In matters of humor, what is appealing to one person may be appalling to another." —Mel Helitzer

"Jokes of the proper kind, properly told, can do more to enlighten questions of politics, philosophy, and literature than any number of dull arguments." —Isaac Asimov

"Where humor is concerned, there are no standards -- no one can say what is good or bad, although you can be sure that everyone will." —John Kenneth Galbraith

Here are the twenty-one PWLOARYK Principles. You now have solid guidelines for mixing work and play in the right way, at the right time, for the right reasons. Follow these principles and you will promote higher levels of health, satisfaction, creativity, and productivity for yourself and those with whom you work.

PRINCIPLE I:
"Fun" is a subjective term.

PRINCIPLE II:
Work cannot always be play, but work can often be fun.

PRINCIPLE III:
While you are developing your sense of humor, it is a good idea to develop your sensitivity to humor.

PRINCIPLE IV:
The key to preventing physical and emotional burnout is balance.

PRINCIPLE V:
A good sense of humor means being able to see the absurd, ludicrous, or laughable side of a situation--it does not have to mean telling jokes.

PRINCIPLE VI:
When we are in humor, or any positive emotion, our brain chemistry changes.

PRINCIPLE VII:

Mixing work and play will be counterproductive when employees are immature, angry, or poorly trained in the value of fun.

PRINCIPLE VIII:

When managers deny employees the opportunity for harmless mixing of work and play, the employees will be resentful and engage in covert play (or sabotage).

PRINCIPLE IX:

All aspects of mixing work and play must be positive.

PRINCIPLE X:

Learn to appreciate the difference between being "stupid" and being "silly."

PRINCIPLE XI:

Mixing work and play works best to moderate minor irritations and to help people to get along better.

PRINCIPLE XII:

Take "humor breaks." Punctuate the work day with opportunities to mix work and play.

PRINCIPLE XIII:

Mixing work and play is voluntary, something you do because you want to, not because you have to.

PRINCIPLE XIV:

Issue invitations for others to join in the fun, don't demand that they participate.

PRINCIPLE XV:

Create opportunities for mixing work and play which take into account individual tastes and needs.

PRINCIPLE XVI:

Organize a group to help get the fun going and ask for suggestions.

PRINCIPLE XVII:

Don't worry about the sourpusses.

PRINCIPLE XVIII:

You don't have to stop being serious to be humorous or to mix work and play.

PRINCIPLE XIX:

Lighten up.

PRINCIPLE XX:

There is a time to laugh and time to cry.

PRINCIPLE XXI:

"Funny" is in the eye of the be-ho-ho-holder.

CHAPTER 4

EIGHTY-NINE PROVEN WAYS TO HAVE FUN AT WORK

"When we provide an environment that is pleasant and multidimensional—fun!—we inspire people. They look at things differently. They become more creative and productive." —Fred Pryor

I have met hundreds of people over the past several years who agree that they would like to have fun at work but they aren't sure of exactly what that means or how to do it. Others have long lists of things they do to stay happy, healthy, and productive on the job. Here are 89 ways to get you started or to add to your repertoire. Use this list as inspiration. These ideas are working for somebody somewhere, but an idea may not work for you in exactly the way it is presented here. Be creative: be prepared to spin-off, piggy-back, extend, adapt, modify, or otherwise change any idea presented here to make it appropriate for your workplace. When you come up with a new way of having fun at work, sent it to me. I will share it with others, and I will send you an "Official Sense of Humor" certificate.

89 WAYS PEOPLE HAVE FUN AT WORK:

1. We rent a video and make popcorn. Then we watch and eat during certain boring, repetitive jobs.

2. We keep an office Polaroid camera which everyone has access to; we post the candid and spontaneous photos.

3. We keep a "Far Side" calendar in the photocopy room so while you wait for your copies you can look at cartoons.

4. We sometimes write outrageous memos in the midst of serious ones.

5. One company newsletter we publish is strictly on the lighter side.

6. Departments perform skits at our Christmas party.

7. Our department is 80 women. Once a year we have an outing to a male strip show.

8. We add "fun" names to things or places at work and on agenda items for meetings.

9. "Chinese" gift exchange is held sometimes for a holiday, sometimes for no reason (items are "opt or swapped").

10. We have "Secret Friend" gift exchanges all through the year.

11. Sometimes an intentionally misunderstood communication breaks the tension.

12. We include a "pearls of wisdom" birthday card at a birthday party. All department members contribute good wishes and a wise saying.

13. We adopt and support local school teams.

14. We use practical jokes and exaggeration humor.

15. We made a music video about the job with the help of our media/communications department. All employees got to ham it up; showed great attitudes.

16. We take breaks we call "pause gymnastics"—with music; it only takes a few minutes.

17. We made a humorous video involving department members.

18. Friday afternoons about 3:30 all work stops and employees gather in the cafeteria for a social break.

19. We take one-minute "massage train" breaks.

20. We give "Foul Weather Friends" Awards to the employees who deal with most difficult customers. They get a certificate and a raincoat!

21. Periodically our executives cook breakfast for everybody.

22. We have potluck dinners.

23. English high tea is held once in a while in our department.

24. We have celebratory meetings for a variety of successes: job well-done, projects completed.

25. We give a "Hang In" award for completion of extra long projects.

26. We go out to lunch together around holidays.

27. We present skits and give a variety of awards.

28. We make up acronyms for humorous incidents.

29. We dress up to impersonate the managers.

30. We hired a caricaturist to draw pictures of us during a meeting.

31. We have popcorn parties.

32. We have weekend family picnics.

33. Our manager surprised us by renting a bus and taking us on a picnic, complete with accordion player and watermelon.

34. We give a "Shark" award for hard work, getting through a hard time.

35. We have Humor/Fun/Joy committees; membership rotates.

36. We go on cruises.

37. We have "dress up" and "dress down" days.

38. We have an "Outrageous Necktie Day" and give prizes.

39. We have "Funny T-shirt Day" or "Funny Hat Day" or "Funny Badge Day." We award prizes for the tackiest, most outrageous, funniest, weirdest, ugliest, etc.

40. We keep a popcorn machine in the office so anyone can pop corn anytime.

41. We held a "Neon Day." Everyone wore something neon and we gave out prizes.

42. We have taken trips to the circus together.

43. Tickets to various cultural and athletic events are great prizes in our department.

44. Part of our Christmas bonus included two movie passes each month for a year.

45. We have a "TOAD-of-the-month" award for the biggest screw-up with the emphasis on learning from the mistake.

46. For us, any event that has food catered is extra special and fun.

47. It is fun to decorate for the holidays throughout the year.

48. From time to time we videotape reports instead of making live presentations.

49. We have rented an amusement park for a day of fun for employees and their families.

50. Employees perform Christmas skits, and to make it more fun we have added an applause meter.

51. We go out for lunch together.

52. We made the rounds of the homes of co-workers at Halloween for "trick-or-drink."

53. We dress up at the office for Halloween.

54. We take "Dysfunctional Breaks"—any break during an overloaded crazy time to relieve the tension.

55. We have played elaborate practical jokes (e.g. moving someone's car from the parking lot and replacing it with a wreck!).

56. We have a "Bring spouse to work day."

57. We have a relaxing "Friday Afternoon Club."

58. We started a "Summer Hours" schedule one year so we could have long weekends. It worked out so well it was extended to year 'round.

59. We instituted a "Bored Friday" social get-together which follows a Friday Board meeting.

60. We held a mini olympics and an office wellness olympics.

61. We have a "Whine-along" in which we sing our complaints about the job to the tunes of familiar songs.

62. We play Team Trivial Pursuit.

63. We have formed hiker's groups among our co-workers (a High Peak group and a Low Peak group depending on the level of hiking one enjoys).

64. We have a contest for "Ties You Wouldn't Wear to IBM."

65. Our employees can present each other with "You Made a Difference" certificates at any time to show appreciation.

66. We ask someone to teach us something about their job.

67. We organize intramural athletic events.

68. We celebrate "Humor Week"—can be done anytime. (National Humor Day is April 15th!)

69. We created a contest in which recent employee photos have to be matched with their baby pictures.

70. We hire a Shiatsu masseuse for 15-minute massages twice a month.

71. We put the names of employees who have earned "Applause" recognition for good effort into a lottery for prizes on a quarterly basis. The more "Applause," the more chances to win.

72. We set aside time during lunch hours on certain days for playing board games in our conference room.

73. I hung an old kitchen cabinet door on the outside of my office door and put a cartoon behind it for others to find when they open the cupboard door. Soon, I found cartoons that were put there by my co-workers. It has become self-perpetuating.

74. We have a volunteer clown troupe made up of seventy co-workers. We hired a professional clown to put on a clown school for us. Now we visit shelters, special schools, and other worthwhile projects.

75. We celebrate New Year's Eve, complete with party and all the trimmings, on April 30, the anniversary of the founding of our company.

76. We keep a toy box in our office full of fun games and props which anyone can use whenever things get tense.

77. When the pressure is on at our office, we take off our shoes and have a short break for a game of barefoot soccer in the hallway.

78. During our executive meetings, I put one person in charge of a "Terminator" sound effects gadget with the instruction to "Zap any bull----anytime you hear it." It keeps us from getting too long-winded and relieves the tension.

79. When we go into a brainstorming session, I pass out giant sponge balls to be thrown at anyone who uses negative "killer" phrases. It keep us positive and productive.

80. If things are getting hectic at our office, we take a break for a jelly-bean fight. Everyone gets armed with a cupful of jelly beans and we fire them at each other. When we've all had a good laugh, we clean up together.

81. I place a stack of $1000.00 bills (phoney) on the conference table at the start of a creativity meeting and "pay off" throughout the meeting for good ideas. Everyone has a good laugh and tries hard to come up with "money-makers."

82. Our Total Quality program emphasizes our mission. When we catch someone "upholding the mission" of the organization, they are rewarded with a certificate and a pair of suspenders.

83. We keep a brass bell in the office which is rung every time we make a sale. When we hear the bell we know something good has just happened and we all feel encouraged to keep on keepin' on.

84. One of our computer programmers has programmed jokes into our mainframe. Every time anyone logs on to their terminal a randomly selected joke appears. The operator has the option of seeing more jokes or getting to work. When we need a break we can ask the computer to show us more jokes.

85. We were getting bored with the same old donuts every Friday, so we instituted a Friday snack rotation, in which each Friday, a different employee in the office brings in treats for the group. The company pays for it and we get quite a variety of goodies.

86. Dominos Pizza conducts an annual Pizza Olympics with local, regional, and national contests, tied to various aspects of the business from pizza making to accounting. There are great prizes, the company gets insight into improving procedures, and everyone has a lot of fun.

87. We taped candy bars to the last page of our quarterly stockholders report.

88. We use a jumbo 22" by 28" pink telephone message pad which reads "MIRTH MEMO" to lighten up the day.

89. We cut pictures of different people out of magazines (especially the gossip tabloids), put them on the bulletin board, and invite everyone in the office to make up captions.

Do you have a way of mixing work and play that wasn't on this list? See *The Last Word*, page 143.

CHAPTER 5

LEGENDARY PWLOARYK

Now you have an idea of the range of activities people get into as they mix work and play successfully. Here are detailed descriptions of companies mixing working and play with outstanding results. As you can see, some of the ideas are easy to implement at practically no cost and they seem to be consistent with the boundaries of taste in most organizations. I have purposely included some of the more elaborate, costly, and outrageous ideas too, as a way of showing you some of the "outer limits" of mixing work and play. My hope is that this mixture of ideas will spark your own creative imagination and you will have the AHA experience, the flash in insight as to how you can invite some HA-HA experiences where you work.

It seems like a good idea to give you more detail than the list of 89 ways can cover. It will be helpful to know more about how organizations incorporate fun into their routines. Therefore, I have polled some of my client organizations which are doing a great job of PWLOARYKing for their stories. These case histories, along with stories which have been newsworthy, and some award-winners, provide greater detail about "how to do it" and show the tremendous impact you can have. With these examples in mind, you can reach your own employees and then extend your reach out into the community (and the world, for that matter).

CASE HISTORY 1. HUMOR ILLUMINATES EDUCATION, SAFETY, ECOLOGY MESSAGES

When I addressed the Women's Guild of Orange and Rockland Utilities in New York State last year, I found a group with a great sense of humor. Under the leadership of James F. Smith and Linda Winikow, and with tremendous support from people like Maria Sclafani and Cecille Drier, they practice mixing work and play with great results in morale and productivity. The video of their Halloween Party showed how an organization can promote fun activities that support and encourage family involvement. As a follow-up I was invited to speak to the Edison Electric Institute which is the national association of America's investor-owned electric utilities.

I learned about the Institute's *Common Goals Awards* as I was researching material in preparation for addressing their Tampa meeting.

WATTS BUGGING KIDS?!

An impressive award winner was "Louie The Lightning Bug." Since 1983, Louie has been making children and adults alike laugh while teaching valuable lessons about electrical safety and now about recycling. Louie first appeared nearly nine years ago in 30-second commercials aimed at children 6-11. After only three months, he achieved a 96% awareness rating among children and well over 80% for adults. The program was developed by Alabama Power Company and is now syndicated to almost 200 utilities in the United States and Canada.

Louie is a lighthearted character easily recognized by his unique voice. An animated Louie flits through numerous commercials with a supporting cast of dancing trees, kites, children and electrical appliances all singing Louie's central message of "You gotta play it safe around electricity." Animation is combined with live action in an adult education spot and ten minute "feature film" which is distributed to elementary schools. Both echo the electrical safety message. In 1990, a new commercial was developed featuring Louie "putting a bug in your ear" about the importance of recycling. Earth Day 1991 was the premier of Louie's latest message.

The green and yellow Louie, who has a light bulb for a tail, teams up with a super cool spider/jazz guitarist to deliver the message "Be cool with cords." The voice of the spider is none other than the infinitely cool Wolfman Jack.

Clever lyrics and animation are trademarks of the campaign. From the fallen power lines who are "feelin' down" to the little girl who "gets the idea" as Louie's tail lights up above her head, humor is an important yet subtle part of this serious campaign.

Thanks to PWLOARYKists Carol Pickens, Pam Moore, and Trey Woodrow at Alabama Power for all the scoop on Louie.

CASE HISTORY 2. REACHING OUT AND TOUCHING THE FUTURE

Another business and education partnership which was fun and productive for all happened in Morristown, New Jersey, and involved employees of AT&T and the Sussex Avenue School. Kim Cutler shared with me this description of the project.

Over 100 employees from AT&T's Communications Services Financial Organization volunteered their time to work with the students and teachers at Sussex Avenue School. The activities ranged from joint work on Science Fair exhibits and history projects (including construction of a 7-foot map of New Jersey) to remedial and enrichment assistance in math and reading.

Volunteers have also been involved in physical education programs and have helped establish a jogging club for students. Additional volunteers have also acted as student mentors for some of the children, serving as role models, tutors, and confidants.

Over 350 students, faculty, and volunteers joined in the end-of-year celebration, enjoying ice cream, cake, balloons, and games on the grounds of the Sussex Avenue School. With several students gathered around, one of the AT&T volunteers commented, "It's sad to see the program come to a close this year, but we are all looking forward to next year!"

Cherie Stowe and Ed Obuchowski from AT&T were the primary organizers of this project, along with Larry Koch, the school principal. Stowe, a District Manager, said, "This has been a remarkable relationship—Larry Koch, Mary Quirk, the peer teacher and all of the faculty have been outstanding to work with. This Partnership Project has provided an excellent opportunity to AT&T to reach out into the community. We are well aware that the workforce of the future is sitting in these classrooms today and I truly believe that with business and education working together, we can achieve some wonderful results."

CASE HISTORY 3. BIOBREAKS: A PIECE OF THE ORTHO BIOTECH CULTURE

I had the pleasure of working with Andrea Zintz, Ph.D., Vice President, Human Resources, at Ortho Pharmaceutical Company's Biotech Division in Raritan, New Jersey. Zintz, thinking and planning for the start-up of Ortho Biotech, visioned a new concept which would foster initial cohesiveness and contribute to the long-term morale of the division. Here, Zintz and Patty Imbriani tell what happened.

"*Biobreaks* came as an inspiration during a strategic planning meeting of our Management Board as we were discussing the stress associated with company start-ups, and the creative things that were going on in small Biotech companies to relieve burnout and stress. We learned from our V.P. of Research that many California-based companies were holding informal Friday afternoon "beer-blasts" to encourage cross-departmental/cross-level networking, and that employees let their hair down with one another in a way that promoted social comfort and new creative ideas applicable on the job.

"We decided that time allocated during working hours on a regular basis to promote informal networking could have the following benefits:

* a needed break from the "nose-to-the-grindstone" atmosphere of a start-up organization
* stress-reduction; greater mental and physical health
* increased creativity through sharing ideas, reactions, and general informal information exchange
* reinforcing the cultural values for teamwork and a climate for positive, inclusive, and informal communication.

"We wanted to name our informal breaks something fun and have the title be connected to the name of our company, Ortho Biotech, so we brainstormed some titles and *Biobreaks* emerged as the winner.

"We also wanted to begin our first *Biobreak* with a tone-setter. A launch-event that would communicate the spirit of Biobreaks along with some relevant messages about teamwork, win-win communication, and humor at work. We enlisted the services of Steve Wilson of DPJ Enterprises, Inc., Columbus, Ohio, for a two-hour *Biobreak* kick-off meeting.

"All of the Board members were in attendance. We used moveable chairs that would permit them to be moved to the perimeter later on for floor activities. Our President kicked the meeting off with an introduction to the concept of Biobreaks, and I introduced Steve Wilson. Steve led with a brief introduction centering on humor and its benefits in the work place, and then led us through some "Playshop" exercises that built on relevant concepts like cooperation, creativity, altering perspectives and nurturing one another.

"The session was a hit! A committee of employees was formed to plan our follow-up events. They decided that *Biobreaks* would be held every Friday from 4:00 to 5:00 p.m. in the Biotech cafeteria. The committee concentrated on ways to ensure that the spirit of the first *Biobreak* was infused onto the others. Every department within Ortho Biotech would get a chance to sponsor a *Biobreak*. Each department's goal was to motivate employees to want to be at their *Biobreak*. This was done through the use of intriguing desk drops or posters which would entice employees. The hosting department was also responsible for refreshments, room arrangements, props, give-aways, etc. All this had to be done with a $500 per *Biobreak* budget, to be incurred by the sponsoring department.

"To offer greater incentive, after the completion of the first round of departmentally hosted *Biobreaks* (a year's time), we held a contest for the best *Biobreak*. Each employee had a vote for the *Biobreak* of their choice, with the winning department members receiving a grand prize especially selected for them.

"Departments became very creative as well as competitive. There were trivia contests, scavenger hunts, dancing, and always plenty of good food. Most of all employees enjoyed the breaks, relaxing, and socializing with co-workers of all levels and departments.

"The workload at Ortho Biotech, as with many other companies, is demanding. It is commonplace for employees to become so engrossed in the work that interacting socially, relaxing, and sharing new ideas can get overlooked. *Biobreaks* help the employees to stop work for a little while, meet those with whom they share a facility and company, and have some fun.

"We started *Biobreaks* a year and a half ago, and have since modified the *Biobreak* schedule so that now we hold them spontaneously, as needed. Any department that wishes to host an event such as a volleyball picnic right after work or a breakfast event need only plan it and advertise the date as an Ortho Biotech *Biobreak*."

This is a good example of how flexibility allows a program to grow and develop to keep up with the changing needs of the organization.

CASE HISTORY 4. A HUMOR ROOM TO FOCUS ON EMPLOYEES' WELL-BEING

With world crises and the national economy heating up, according to a February 19, 1991 *Wall Street Journal* report, "businesses are turning to laughter to put their problems in perspective." While the grinning of corporate America remains quite a challenge, the use of humor consultants and the spread of humor education are paying off with some surprising innovations. How about a "humor task force" and a "humor room"?

That is exactly what Lindsay Collier is cooking up at Eastman Kodak Co., to help stimulate creative thinking, relieve chronic uptightness, and improve communications. I heard about these developments from Collier, a 24-year Kodak veteran, and technical adviser to a Kodak management services division that, among other things, is studying creativity, innovation and strategic exploration. "When people are laughing and enjoying themselves," says Collier, "they can be creative. When they're not, they probably aren't."

Garnering encouragement and ideas from a "humor support group" of 40 people from various Kodak departments, he has designed a series of humor rooms. The first is expected to open officially in October of 1991, at the company's Kodak Park location in Rochester, New York. Lindsay plans other humor rooms to be located to give easier access to employees at four different locations. He plans to bring the power of humor to manufacturing, research, and administrative employees next.

Among its many offerings, the 20-foot-by-50-foot humor room will be stocked with Monty Python and Candid Camera videos, Dave Barry and Woody Allen books, and a variety of props to stimulate, relax, and help employees to lighten up. The room will have four main sections: (1) a publications and media resource center, (2) a High-Tech area with personal computers and off-the-shelf software which employees can use to write their own jokes or stimulate creativity, (3) a Presentation area, loaded with audio-visual equipment, with some videos running throughout the day, and (4) a "Toy Store" with an ample supply of props and gags like Groucho glasses and wind-up chattering teeth, costumes, juggling supplies, and a 5-foot tall Saddam Hussein punching bag.

Collier envisions humor projects such as collecting audio recordings of employee's laughter (for playback at a later date), and "ideation sessions." "My informal research," Collier told me, "shows that people say they are most creative while driving, brushing their teeth, showering, or sitting on the commode. So, of course, plans call for the humor room to stimulate creativity by having a steering wheel, fake shower, tooth brushes, and a 'creativity commode' (non-working)."

Whether the room is used as a place to let off (or laugh off) tensions, or it becomes a library of resources on humor and creativity, the concept underscores a phenomenal—and happy—change for corporate employees. Teaching workers to reach for laughs instead of tranquilizers is a very healthy move. Companies whose executives have not been known for being a barrel of laughs are recognizing the importance of the balance that comes with healthy humor. If businesses heed the advice of humor consultants, they will, as Dana Milbank pointed out in the *Wall Street Journal* report, "give up their old-boy humor with its reliance on sexism, racism, and put-downs" and, instead, opt for "making fun of oneself instead of others, spontaneity and jokes about common problems."

CASE HISTORY 5. HUMOR IN RETAILING: RIGHT ON TARGET

"You can't have a fun environment to shop in if you don't have a fun environment to work in." That is the philosophy of Nancy Robbins, Manager of Management and Organizational Development for Target Stores, a division of Dayton Hudson Corporation, Minneapolis, Minnesota. With that concept in mind, since 1988, Robbins has developed and instituted humor training programs for managers, current employees, and new hires. Since 1988, more than 10,000 employees have requested and completed some aspect of the humor training, making it the most popular training offered by the organization, which has 463 stores in 32 states. Humor training and training with humor has paid off for Target in several important ways.

Based on a concept originated by Larry Gilpin, Senior Vice President of Personnel, the company's vision for the 90's and beyond is to be known as "the fast, fun, and friendly place" to work and shop. After studying the fun training techniques used by Disney, Robbins designed humor training programs that blend a party atmosphere with serious purposes. The program for new employees is called "Target University" and consists of a four-hour workshop bolstering self-esteem and boosting employees' ability to handle customer service challenges with finesse while diverting stress and avoiding burnout.

Target University welcomes participants to the strains of Patti LaBelle's *I've Got A New Attitude.* Then they are exposed to a fast-paced, fun-filled program that includes off-the-shelf videos which use humor to drive home important techniques for avoiding customer service nightmares, special sessions on schmoozing and smiling, and ways to create "make it" moments that enhance customer service. "One of the important goals of the training," says Robbins, "is to build habits that will continue." (Used with permission)

The Humor Perspective is the name of another of Robbins' training pieces, designed especially for Target managers. Like Target University, this 90-minute program has also been in place for three years and enjoys enormous popularity. The idea is to develop positive humor skills in the managers. They can then support the graduates of Target University and act as role models of managing stress by using humor to balance perspective, and dealing with customers in a positive frame of mind.

POSITIVE OUTCOMES

Beyond the sheer popularity of the training among employees, highly desirable results show up in customer satisfaction surveys and turnover rates. An analysis of "Let Me Know" customer comment cards shows that the number of positive comments has steadily increased, "quarter by quarter," since humor training was instituted in 1988, while the number of negative comments has steadily dropped. The company has also experienced a steady decline in employee turnover in the same period. While Robbins realizes that Target University doesn't get all of the credit for these improvements, she does believe, and I agree, that humor training provides conscious, positive support for company goals and accomplishments. With results like these, it is impossible not to go for the obvious pun: Target is on target with humor!

CHAPTER 6

T.Q.I.F--TOTAL QUALITY IS FUN (OR IT SHOULD BE!)

An editorial by Chris Lee in the September, 1990 *Training Magazine* carried this eye-opening observation about a problem in Douglas Aircraft's attempt to instill a new participative corporate culture:

> Despite the fact that employees are now called *teammates* noted a recent report in the *New York Times*, 'the [new] philosophy has not taken with all employees, some of who refer to TQMS [Total Quality Management System] as *Time To Quit and Move to Seattle*, the home of arch rival Boeing.' Meanwhile, management scratches its head, wondering why it's so hard to motivate such a recalcitrant group of *teammates*.

Recalcitrant??? Now that you have been following the findings about how PWLOARYK is such an important application of psychology and humor to work, you could probably diagnose a key part of the problem. You might have deduced that an element of fun makes new programs much more attractive; that humorless teams aren't teams for very long; that hard-driven, dogged application of even the best ideas, if not balanced with some lightness periodically, fosters physical and emotional burnout. How many times do we have to say it: all work and no play means Jack's company isn't as productive as it could be.

The national quality improvement push begun about 10 years ago in this country was--and still is--sorely needed. This non-traditional approach, applying quality improvement principles way beyond assembly line post-production inspections, to include everybody's products from the CEO on down to the janitor, is dynamite. Too often, however, the American way of working is overly solemn, dull and matter-of-fact, or just too intense. Of course, some of the most productive and profitable companies know better. They know that non-traditional programs call for non-traditional implementation: they make it FUN. Fun, of course, does not mean turning work into a circus. But, as creativity expert Roger von Oech puts it, "The fun is contagious and everybody works harder to get a piece of that fun."

Sociologist John Bowman, Management Professor David Abramis, and Management Consultant Fred Pryor have all indicated that we need to take a closer look at our traditional beliefs about concepts such as "play," "fun," "satisfaction," and "joking on the job." Accessing the power of these dimensions appropriately, we improve teamwork, employee health, morale, creativity, productivity, and job satisfaction. Here are four examples of an aspect of the quality improvement programs in which *appropriate fun* is being applied successfully.

Example 1: I saw a wonderful application of PWLOARYK psychology during Quality Day in Augusta, Georgia, conducted for 400 employees and associates of the Westinghouse Savannah River Company where I had the pleasure of being invited to present some ideas about "Humor and Stress and Stress In The Workplace." The development and structure of the Westinghouse Total Quality program is indeed impressive. The balanced attitude of the Savannah River Site executives who are responsible for making the TQ program operational was gratifying.

Under the leadership of J. W. "Walt" Joseph, Andy Workum and Lisa Allen developed a recognition and encouragement program called MVP. Playing off of the familiar Most Valuable Player award in sports and the three pillars of TQ called Mission, Vision, and Principles, they invented a triangle-shaped printed memo form. In LARGE letters it says "Thanks For Being An MVP" and there is space on the form for telling a fellow employee in writing why you think s/he is an MVP. The recognition is taken a step further because the form has a carbonless copy attached and a copy of the MVP recognition is sent to the employee's supervisor.

Walt Joseph and his team had fun creating MVP. Their enthusiasm, like all good humor and fun, is contagious. They are demonstrating that peer recognition is fun. Catching people doing the right things and letting them know it is fun. It is fun for supervisors to receive MVP reports on members of their work group. Consciousness about TQ is raised and everyone stays focused (there is even a clever reprint of the structure for TQ Conditions of Excellence on the MVP form).

Example 2: Al Grorud is CFO and heads up the Systems Development Organization within the Information Management System of AT&T. He is openly enthusiastic and a strong supporter of an effort called the APPLAUSE program. The company invites peer recognition for individual contributions as a part of the mix of factors they use to foster overall quality improvement. The program "plusses" this concept by entering the names of employees receiving APPLAUSE awards into a drawing for additional prizes. That's what I call extending the focus.

Grorud promotes balanced PWLOARYK for executives, too. Based on his needs assessment, I created a highly interactive and playful program for achieving some very important goals during a CFO weekend retreat in the Poconos. A group of fifty financial officers and their "significant others" participated in a Playshop aimed at helping them better understand one another and enhance teamwork, while promoting a new understanding of how PWLOARYK could help them deal with both personal and job stress. It was a huge success. The executives and their spouses had a great time, and they took home information that was potentially life-saving.

Example 3: Elyria Memorial Hospital in Elyria, Ohio, created a certificate with a similar peer recognition purpose for their "YOU MADE A DIFFERENCE" program. Following a presentation about

"Putting Humor To Work At Work," Jim Imler, Assistant Vice President, Personnel Services, and other management staff commented that the "YOU MADE A DIFFERENCE" program has added the right light touch to the otherwise pressured and highly demanding responsibilities of a hospital staff.

Example 4: The Edison Electric Institute is the national association of America's investor-owned electric utilities. I learned about the Institute's *Common Goals Awards* as I was preparing to address their Tampa meeting in 1991. One of the award winners, The Cleveland Electric Illuminating Company, developed an outstanding educational partnership with a school. I recognized it as a good example of PWLOARYK.

As a part of Cleveland, Ohio's educational reform to increase the number of high school graduates, Cleveland Electric Illuminating entered an educational partnership with Glenville High School, an inner-city school with 1,200 students facing major problems with attendance, a high drop-out rate, and poor attitudes toward education among both students and teachers.

Using a management-by-objective approach to increase attendance, attention was given to "The Three A's," *Attitude, Achievement, and Attendance.* "Each element," they said, "had numerous plans of action. Our basic premise was that kids will do what is fun even if they won't do what isn't. It worked well." Cleveland Electric employees were actively involved and support was given by local media.

They made Freshman Orientation fun by offering prize drawings, refreshments, and football tickets. Attendance jumped from 4 in 1988 to 190 in 1989. Teacher's in-service days became Pizza Party Days. Attendance jumped from 0 in 1988 to 100 in 1989. "Everyone enjoys fun," they observed and, "we met the big objective. Overall attendance in 1989 was up to 80%. That represented a 4% or 5% gain over the previous downward trend.

WHAT LEVEL OF QUALITY?

As American business sets its sights on recovering a leading position in competitive excellence, the inevitable questions arise. What quality standard is acceptable? Considering our imperfect nature and the ubiquitous presence of human foibles, what margin of error in our work will we allow? If we cut ourselves some slack, won't we be less stressed about the whole thing? How can mixing work and play improve our quality outcomes? The highest possible level at which we can set standards of quality is 100 percent—error-free, defect-free, in the delivery of goods and services to both external and internal customers. Is this possible? What are the consequences of settling for less than perfection?

Natalie Gabel, working as an intern for *TRAINING Special Projects*, combed a number of solid sources for answers as she prepared a March, 1991, report, "Is 99.9% Good Enough?" For one thing, she found that, at least in some cases, a quality standard goal of 100% is attainable. She reported, "A Hewlett-Packard study of 300,000 semiconductors from three American firms and three Japanese firms recently found the average failure rate of the American chips was over 0.2 percent; the failure rate for Japanese-made chips was zero."

TALLY-HA!

Based on the scale at which we do business and provide products for world markets, even a 0.1 percent error rate—what Gabel calls "almost but not quite"—produces huge problems. Consider that these are some of the results we would get if 99.9 percent were good enough:

* Two million documents will be lost by the IRS this year.
* 811,000 faulty rolls of 35 mm film will be loaded this year.
* 22,000 checks will be deducted from the wrong bank accounts in the next 60 minutes.
* 1,314 phone calls will be misplaced by telecommunications services every minute.
* 12 babies will be given to the wrong parents each day.
* 3,056 copies of tomorrow's *Wall Street Journal* will be missing one of the three sections.
* 20,000 incorrect drug prescriptions will be written in the next twelve months.
* 880,000 credit cards in circulation will turn out to have incorrect cardholder information on their magnetic strips.
* 18,322 pieces of mail will be mishandled in the next hour.

HOW STRESS AFFECTS QUALITY

One theory—which I believe stands a good chance of being substantiated through careful research—holds that brain chemistry changes during stress, causing us to make more mistakes than when we are relaxed.

According to this theory, when we get uptight, frustrated, or too intense, a part of the brain called the *limbic system* starts to shut down. The limbic system is a collection of nerves that are associated with connecting and integrating the functions of both halves of our brains. When you are stressed out, your brain does not function as well and you make mistakes; you drop things, spill things, forget names and phone numbers, and lock your keys in the car. When you are relaxed and the limbic system is more active, your "whole brain" is working and you think more clearly, and are less likely to make mistakes.

Humor, laughter, and other positive emotions have the effect of discharging emotional tension, relaxing the mind and body. It makes sense then, that mixing work and play will be a key strategy for attaining total quality. Whether you aspire to win the Malcolm Baldridge National Quality Award, or just want to grow your business on a solid reputation for quality, it is vital to foster a PW-LOARYK attitude.

GO AFTER SOME LAUGHTER

There are hundreds of opportunities to inject *the right fun at the right time* in support of quality improvement programs. Tom Peters says, "In general, a spirited environment is marked by laughter—enthusiasm for being on a team—and trying darn near anything to make the service or product better." The key is to remember that having fun doesn't mean you aren't serious about your goals. Too often, however, the idea of adding fun is overlooked or misapplied, as was possibly the case at Douglas Aircraft.

Some PWLOARYK tips to keep in mind as you develop an overall quality improvement program:

1. Build in a program for recognition and reward.
2. Build in a strong *peer* recognition component.
3. "Fun" means *different* things to different people; appeal to different "senses" of fun.
4. Issue invitations—not demands—to employees to join the fun.
5. Sometimes it pays to be serious about fun.

Westinghouse's Savannah River Company, AT&T's SMO Division, Elyria Memorial Hospital, and Cleveland Electric Illuminating are examples of companies with the right idea.

CHAPTER 7

THE "UH-OH SQUAD," A WORKPLACE INNOVATION

According to T. George Harris and Robert Trotter, in a report in the March, 1989 *Psychology Today,* "You don't have to work like a dog to get more done. Build your effectiveness on play and fantasy." The report heralded "The new American worker . . . driven by finding gratification in the job itself." They saw evidence that "the work-for-money-only model had already eroded by the late '60s." They said that "It seems a bit odd to suggest that to boost productivity you might work less and play more. But the human spirit, strangely and wondrously made, always turns out to be a surprise."

In a related report, organizational psychologist and consultant David Abramis, Ph.D., California State University at Long Beach, presented some of his research findings about job satisfaction, work, and play. In one of his studies, 341 men and women were asked, "What would make your job more fun?" A number of people said, "Get rid of my supervisor." The responses of participants in my humor seminars give strong indication of the presence of negative supervisors on the job. It amounts to a significant problem in America today. At my seminars, during Question & Answer sessions, the most frequently asked question is, "What can I do about my negative boss?" I have a PWLOARYK answer.

THE PROBLEMS WITH NEGATIVE SUPERVISORS

A "negative boss" is one who shows very little sense of humor. He or she does not roll with the punches when there are problems. They yell, belittle their subordinates, and generally take out their frustrations on everyone within earshot. They are grim, overly serious, and react with anger and fierceness when things go wrong. They are not role-models of a balanced perspective. They act in ways that do not honor the imperfection, value, and vulnerability of the employees. Based on the descriptions I have received, there are plenty of these "Scrooges" and "Grinches" out in the world of work, and they are stealing health, satisfaction, and productivity from their employees and their businesses. There are four serious problems which develop around these kinds of bosses.

(1) FAILURE TO REPORT PROBLEMS: If a supervisor reacts strongly with negatives when things go wrong, workers, fearing that wrath, will avoid reporting problems. This shows up as broken equipment which is put back in the supply closet rather than turned in for repair, or passing problem documents and customers' complaints from worker to worker, like hot potatoes. By the time the problem is discovered, it is much more time-consuming and costly to repair than if it had been reported immediately.

(2) WORRIED SICK: Negative bosses have a way of transferring their hostility, impatience, and intolerance to their employees. It shows up in the workers as anxiety, worry, and stress. Because of the way the mind and body are connected, it is literally possible to be "worried sick" about the boss's reaction, causing a worker to need one or more days of sick leave. It is almost impossible to completely make up for the lost productivity due to having to take time off from work.

(3) NO NEW LEARNING: The way our brains work, it is easiest for us to absorb and retain new information when we are in a positive frame of mind. When an angry supervisor berates an employee and then tries to teach him how to correct a problem, the lesson is wasted. The negativity of the boss is transferred to the worker and part of the worker's brain will not function to learn the new information. Then the next time the problem arises--and there will certainly be a next time--the worker is no better prepared to solve it than he was the first time.

(4) REDUCED MORALE AND TEAMWORK: Any time negative attitudes are present from the leadership or management of an organization, the workers are less motivated to produce. When employees are fearful or resentful, work gets sloppy, the error rate increases, communication breaks down, and sabotage occurs.

THE "UH-OH SQUAD" SOLUTION

Considering all this a few years ago, I invented a solution for overcoming negativity at work when we are faced with the daily minor irritations: The UH-OH Squad. For years, I have distributed "UH-OH Squad" equipment to workers all across North America. I shall continue to do so. It is my mission to improve the lives of workers everywhere by forming "UH-OH Squads."

"UH-OH" situations happen every day. You know you are in an "UH-OH" situation because you get a certain feeling in the pit of your stomach and a voice in your head says, "UH-OH." These are signals of impending stress. If you don't do something constructive, your brain chemistry will change, you will begin to lose your usual clear thinking, worry will set in, followed by reduced effectiveness and, possibly, illness. Now you can counteract the "UH-OHs" by forming a squad in your department at work. Here is how you do it.

The official equipment for squad members is a red sponge rubber clown nose. Obtain equipment for each member of the squad. Issue each squad member their personal equipment. They should keep it at-the-ready in a desk drawer or locker. Then whenever anyone working in your department finds themselves in an "UH-OH" situation, they issue the "UH-OH Alert": "*I need the UH-OH Squad!!!*" Everyone who hears the alert stops whatever they are doing (this only takes about 30 seconds), gets their equipment--clown noses--and gathers around the person who issued that alert. They all put on the equipment, stand around the person and the problem and, together, chant four times, "UH-OH! UH-OH! UH-OH! UH-OH!" with great mock bewilderment.

WHY IT WORKS

The response of the squad, the red noses, the group effort, and the ensuing laughter all combine to help you pull together rather than fall apart in the face of problems. What you actually create is a combination of psychological "anchors" to remind you to keep your perspective in balance, take a deep breath, feel the support of the group, solve the problem, stay healthy, and keep on being productive.

You can't always get rid of your supervisor, but you can still have fun and maintain productivity on the job with innovations such as the "UH-OH Squad." Over the years I have received a great deal of testimony about the effectiveness of "UH-OH Squads." Of course, not everyone is in a position at work to don a clown nose or gather 'round to chant "UH-OHs." In those cases, I have been told, once the concept is understood, merely saying the word "Uh-Oh" brings peals of laughter and relaxation as everyone is reminded to lighten up. This way of mixing work and play has proven effective in hundreds of situations in dozens of businesses, schools, and hospitals. You can do it too!

CHAPTER 8

HUMOR POWERED CLASSROOMS

Some people don't work in offices, factories, hospitals, or showrooms; they work in schools and classrooms--the birthplaces of "homework." These are the places where we shape the minds of the young and produce the citizens, parents, and workers who will shape the future of this country and the world.

What good would it do to combine play with schoolwork? Well, as it turns out, there is a great deal to gain by PWLOARYKing in school. Associate Professor of Education, Claudia E. Cornett, says, "Humor has something to offer each of us as we work with children of all ages and abilities. Humor can be used to help correct reading problems, control behavioral disorders, build vocabulary, teach foreign languages, and integrate social isolates. Humor can be one of the most powerful instructional resources." And, as is true for combining work and play anywhere else, there are some guidelines for teachers to keep in mind.

MEMORIES OF ELEMENTARY LAUGHTER

Two memories of my elementary school days flashed through my brain when an elementary school teacher at an in-service training session raised her hand and asked, "What should I do when all the kids in my class are cracking up with laughter and it's getting to be too much? I'm afraid they will get out of control, and then they won't be able to concentrate on their lessons." The other teachers in the training group nodded in silent understanding. The looks on their faces told me that they all were familiar with that kind of giggling, cackling, irrepressible outburst. I had participated in scenes like that when I was in elementary school, and I wondered if they had too.

The first memory evoked by this question had to do with a teacher who tried to put limits on laughter, and got still more laughter as a result. It happened when I was in third grade. I was president of my class, and one of my duties was to take the daily attendance row by row and call aloud the absences to Mrs. Marcowitz, who then would record them in her black book. Then I read to the class the announcements which had come hot from the mimeograph machine in the principal's office that morning. Invariably, the class clown, Jay Zlotnick (who was later to become my "best friend"), would be cutting up somehow, making me laugh and giggle my way through my tasks.

One morning it got to be more giggly than usual and Mrs. Marcowitz rose up from her desk, angry. Actually, it wasn't so much of a rise as it was her sliding off of her chair because she was short and squat. However, in her sturdy oxford shoes she was still taller than most of us and, with her gray hair pulled back in its bun and with rimless glasses framing her grimace, to us she was quite fearsome. She ordered the laughing to halt. Then she ordered Jay to get under the kneehole of the desk (one of her favorite punishments) and stay there while she finished her deskwork and he had learned his lesson. We were properly terrified and silent. But not for long.

Jay was humiliated by her treatment of him and definitely did not like being put under her desk. He had not been there more than three minutes when Mrs. Marcowitz yelped and leapt up from her chair, hopping around the room in pain, losing all composure. Jay had decided to show his displeasure by biting her hard on the ankle. I know we all laughed even more hysterically at her discomfiture but I can't remember what happened after that. Whatever it was, I don't think it was too bad. Jay and I are still friends and we still laugh about the wild scene in third grade.

In the fifth grade I experienced a different version of high comedy and hysterical silliness, with a different reaction from the teacher. While attending the William Cullen Bryant Elementary School, Jay Kirschner and I (both of us influenced by radio comedy and early TV) wrote several humorous skits, which our teacher allowed—even encouraged—us to perform in front of the class.

During one such performance, we just couldn't seem to keep a straight face. We cracked each other up, choking on our own laughter, so much that we could barely get the words out. I remember hearing my own high-pitched cackling. It was the kind that drove my mother up the wall, but I could not stop. Tears streaming down our cheeks, sides aching, Jay and I were unable to read from the scripts we had scribbled on lined tablet paper the night before (I had never earned a grade higher than "U"—which stood for Unsatisfactory—in Handwriting anyway and our hysterical giggling just made matters worse). All of my classmates were breaking up with laughter too, and it all escalated very rapidly.

Oddly, I cannot recall the teacher's reaction and, although I have a vague remembrance of what the skit was about, I have no idea what it was that we thought was so funny. This is probably because what really mattered at the time was just having fun and impressing the other kids. But something magical happened that day which has taken me years to understand. Now I know it as an important part of the psychology of mixing work and play.

There, in my fifth grade classroom, doubled over with joyous laughter, my bladder on the verge of emptying right there in front of everyone, I became completely caught up in the joy of the moment and was lost in the euphoriant effect of laughter. I was so "high" that for some moments I was not aware of anything or anyone other than my own sheer delight. My laughter seemed to be coming from someplace far away as I became lost in a blissful rush of innocence and endorphins. All too soon the scene became quiet, everything snapped back into focus, and we finished the skit. I had definitely lost control but, apparently, my teacher did not stop me from laughing.

WHOSE CLASSROOM IS IT, ANYWAY?

Based on these and other school experiences, and later experiences in the world of work, I have come to recognize that some teachers and parents (and some supervisors and bosses) don't feel that they are really "in charge" unless they interfere with—and call a halt to—such spontaneous expressions of mirth.

As I responded to the teacher's question in the training session, I didn't want my answer to support a general call-to-arms teachers-have-to-exert-authority-over-outbursts thinking. So, in my extemporaneous answer I indicated that the "problem" of laughter in the classroom depends on how often it happens. If this is a low-frequency behavior, occurring, say, three times a year, then I wouldn't consider it a problem which required intervention. I explained that the kids might actually be doing themselves some good by using the natural, tension-reducing effects of laughter to relieve some stress that they might be feeling. We might try to understand what the stress or pressure was, I said. When I could see most of the training group nodding in agreement I thought I had disposed of the question.

But, as sometimes happens, the question wouldn't go away. In the hours which followed the training session, I found myself going through what, over the years, has become a familiar and very helpful process of "personal debriefing." This is when I mentally review a program I have just presented to see where I could have done better. Sometimes my wife has to remind me that I am a very harsh critic of my own work. More often, through this process, I can spot ways to improve my next program and I make notes about what to do differently—better—next time.

The question about the uncontrolled outbursts of young children in class kept coming back to me. I wanted a better answer, something more complete than what the brief Question & Answer period had allowed. For many years, I have been pleasantly taken with the notion that it would be a positive achievement if I could live life in such a way that others would accuse me of having "too much fun." The concept intrigued me. What on earth was "too much" fun, anyway? (And how, exactly, might I go about having it?)

The question of when and how to interfere with the laughter of children deserved careful attention.

WHERE DID YOU GET YOUR SENSE OF HUMOR?

In my own childhood family, the concept of "too much fun" was linked to a sort of ancient guilt trip and superstition. "Laugh before breakfast, cry before supper" was one of my grandmother's ideas. "Don't be too happy about good times or you will surely bring on trouble" was another warning I heard from my elders. It is such ways of thinking that frighten and control us—and they are just not true. These ideas damage our self-esteem by telling us that perhaps we don't deserve the good things that happen to us, or at least, we don't deserve happiness for any extended length of time. And they imply, when they don't say so directly, that such fragile and short-lived happiness might actually be God's will for us. Sadly, after more than twenty-five years of practicing psychotherapy, I see that this kind of thinking is quite common in our society. The simple question about children's laughter in school was beginning to have some profound implications.

How do I see it now? What have I learned from study and observation and from living for fifty years? I absolutely believe that no one should ever feel guilty for feeling happy. Pleasure is our birthright. It is true that not everything is funny, and there is tragedy and sadness in life, but I believe God intends joy for us more than anything else. A rabbi told me that there is an ancient scriptural writing that warns us that when we meet God we are going to be held accountable for not taking greater advantage of the many wonderful things put here for us. Imagine that! The bounty and beauty of this world is put here for our pleasure and we have a responsibility to enjoy life. In Buddhism, it is said that the beginning of wisdom—of understanding the meaning of life—is manifested by a smile, not weeping. When we truly understand why we are here on earth we won't wail and moan. When we "get it" we will be laughing. It is said that "the halls of heaven ring with laughter of the saints," "Even the gods love a joke," and "Laughter is the natural sound of childhood."

A study conducted by Dr. Dolf Zillmann at Indiana University, and reported by Susan Goodman in *CURRENT HEALTH*, January, 1989, found that children learn better and remember more when lessons are mixed with laughter. "For one thing," she points out, "humor keeps their attention focused upon the material. Also, everybody is more willing to enter into an activity if they think they are going to have a good time."

These notions have helped me to understand the laughter of children. Now I can offer a more complete answer to the question that had been nagging at me.

We are apt to engage in mirthful, prolonged, irrepressible outbursts of laughter at any developmental stage—not only in childhood. I have often seen adults doing this. I do it myself from time to time, as does my father, now in his 82nd year. Perhaps you do it, too; who hasn't? It is actually quite satisfying somehow, even if your sides hurt, the tears are streaming down your face, you fall into a limp pile on the carpet, and you can't seem to catch your breath for a moment.

WHAT'S SO FUNNY?

Among humor "academicians," theorists who are far more seriously research-minded than I, there is much speculation as to why we laugh in the first place, and why we can't seem to repress laughter under certain circumstances. However, it is important for teachers to distinguish uncontrollable laughter from irrepressible laughter; healthful, mirthful laughter from malignant or pathological laughter. The uncontrollable type can be chemically induced; there are intoxicants and poisons which have this effect. There are also several psychiatric and neurological conditions in which this kind of laughter is a characteristic symptom. But such is not usually the case with the children in classrooms.

If the children are laughing long and hard, it is important for the teacher or parent to make an assessment before interrupting. Criteria have been developed that can help to differentiate "true/mirthful" or "everyday" laughter that should be permitted and encouraged, from "pathological/malignant" laughter, which signals a need for adult intervention and guidance. Here is what to look for:

(1) If laughter is contagious, sounds warm and inviting, it is probably "true/mirthful" and likely to be healthful. It is not uncommon to hear this kind of laugh and feel like smiling or laughing yourself, even when it comes from another room and you haven't seen "what's funny." However, observers report that laughter associated with pathology has a hollow, shallow sound and others do not readily join in.

(2) In true/mirthful laughter there is usually a build up of some kind of tension (tension builds during the telling of a joke, for instance, if it is done well) and the laughter eventually leaves one with a sense of relief or release, a "whew, that felt good" or "I really needed that" feeling. To the contrary, in pathological/malignant laughter, the laugher reports a build up of tension but no sense of relief or release. Because the person laughing does not experience a reduction of tension, they have no sense of being refreshed or relaxed.

(3) When compared to pathological/malignant laughter, true/mirthful laughter would not be hostile, aggressive, spiteful, or malicious. Laughter at another person's expense, laughter that is offensive and derisive of physical, racial, ethnic, or other inherent characteristics is not the true/mirthful type. In these cases, adult intervention and guidance would be appropriate; e.g., teach children "the 5-minute rule": Do not poke fun at something that another person could not change in the next five minutes.

(4) Even if adults don't "get the joke" that causes children's laughter, if it is the true/mirthful type, careful observation usually reveals the source of the humor in the objective reality; i.e., we can "see" that something has happened to which the children are reacting. On the other hand, pathological/malignant laughter has little or no such observable stimulus in objective reality—perhaps because it is chemically induced or the result of an hallucination. (A word of caution about this criterion: many laughter experts hold that even some true/mirthful laughter is irrational in the sense that we cannot always account for our laughter. We don't always have a "reason" for laughing, or need one; a quite normal experience for many people.)

(5) In addition to serving psychological and physiological functions of reducing tension, true/mirthful laughter is a *self-limiting behavior*. That is, once we start, we have a built-in mechanism which stops us when we've had enough. It's part of the miracle of who we are. No one has ever laughed "forever." Although at the time you might feel like you will never stop, eventually you do. We all do. "Self-limiting" means you never have to tell another person to stop laughing. They will when they're ready, when they've done enough. Isn't that wonderful? Let people "be" when they are laughing and they (through nature or God) will take care of themselves. Give support but don't interfere, and a natural healing process will take place. Interfere and you cut off the process. The "unfinished business" then gets terribly bottled up, draining the person's psychic energy, and reducing their ability to be fully effective and joyful, perhaps for a lifetime.

In summary, it is important to be aware that there is laughter which is healthy, positive, and a sign of mirth and there is laughter which is negative, unhealthy, a sign of illness. The former should be permitted and encouraged; the latter should be discouraged or interrupted. In some cases you should consider making a referral to a physician. Here is a summary of guidelines for knowing which is which.

"GOOD" LAUGHTER	"BAD" LAUGHTER
1. True, mirthful.	1. Forced, pressured.
2. Contagious, warm-sounding.	2. Shallow, hollow sound.
3. Others join in spontaneously.	3. Others don't join in
4. Ends with a sense of relief or of release.	4. Build up of tension but no sense relief.

5. Positive, constructive, uplifting.
6. Can see "what's funny."
7. Self-limiting; stops itself in minutes

5. Hostile, spiteful, malicious, ridicule.
6. Nothing "funny" in objective reality.
7. Virtually unstoppable, may go on for hours.

HUMOR-POWERED CLASSROOMS

Children in classrooms are being natural. As long as their laughter is mirthful and healthful, we should not call it uncontrollable and don't need to feel compelled to interfere. At certain stages of development it may be "bathroom" words or "sex" words or other forbidden talk that creates the emotional tension which triggers the need for release through giddy laughter. Or the children might be sharing a joke which strikes them silly and is entirely invisible to the "adult" sense of humor. So what if the adults don't "get the joke"? When the laughter is mirthful and healthful, let 'em laugh.

Most people agree that the best teachers they ever had in school were not the overly-serious sourpusses, but the ones that made them laugh. The Book of Proverbs tells us, "A wise teacher will teach with joy." "In all this doing and learning," says John-Rogers, "let's not forget one of the most important lessons of all: enjoyment." Teachers from kindergarten to college attend my workshops to learn how to apply psychology and humor for more effective classroom instruction. The following are examples from both ends of the spectrum, along with some thoughts about "good" and "bad" laughter.

FOR LITTLE STUDENTS

Mimi Brodsky Chenfeld of Columbus, Ohio, is an extraordinary teacher, writer, and national consultant with whom I share a mutual admiration and a definite attitude about the importance of humor for young children. In her article *My Loose Is Tooth: Kidding Around With The Kids*, (*Young Children*, November, 1990), she offers humor powered advice to parents and teachers. "(By being) experimental, light-hearted, kidding, reassuring, we can," she says, "be role models, inspirations to our children as we demonstrate through our behavior and our own freedom of speech how to minimize tensions with a joke, how to loosen uptight, closed-in thinking systems with good natured joking, rearranging, challenging, as we help children expand comprehension, build confidence, and enjoy the learning process."

Chenfeld elaborates, "REMEMBER: only in safe environments that are warm, encouraging, open, flexible, stimulating, and accepting will young children express their free-spirited responses to the world around them and to the feelings within them. In silent, strict, overly structured, formalized settings that place little value on talking, playing, and kibitzing, children quickly learn to stifle their ideas and emotions.

"When children learn in fun-filled, loving programs, they easily follow their natural instincts. Because the adults who care for them design many opportunities for talking together, observations and feelings are freely shared. For example, excited Kevin pointed to his teeth and shouted the big news—'My loose is tooth!' "

Among her prescriptions: create a humor collage on a bulletin board. Color it with bright designs; pepper it with cartoons and jokes; add funny faces, silly shapes, incongruous scenes; dot it with riddles and questions and quotes from both the children and the teacher. Surround it with spaces in the room where children can play. "As they play, they have a lot to say—serious and funny things—in the important business of learning.

"Line your shelves with many books to read to the children (such as *The Napping House* (Wood & Wood) or *The King Who Rained* (Gwynne)). Provide many opportunities for talking together—making plans, asking questions, sharing wonder, reviewing information, mixing and matching and mix-ups, brainstorming and open-ended problem solving, encouraging observations, making connections, seeing relationships .,,.,,.,,the list is endless."

HIGHER HUMOR EDUCATION

Education Professor Diana Hunn, at Akron University, is winning support from fellow educators as well as would-be teachers in her classes as she campaigns to send cartoons and comic strips to the head of the class as valuable teaching tools.

Hunn, a seasoned educator, says, "The basis for many cartoons is that you have to understand the science (or vocabulary, or history, or arithmetic, etc.) before you get the joke. So, indirectly, while comic strips and cartoons are reinforcing learning concepts, they also tell kids that learning is fun and a part of our everyday lives. That's the same message teachers try to get through to their pupils."

Here is an example of how it can work. "A comic strip by Roz Chast that appeared in *The New Yorker* magazine starts out with a drawing of a unicycle, then a bicycle, and progresses through a tricycle, a 'quadricycle,' and a 'decacycle.' By the end of the strip the reader is confronted with a vehicle that's virtually all wheels called an 'impossicycle.'

"If you're teaching prefixes to kids, that's a great way to illustrate the lesson. The next step is to initiate a creative exercise, like telling the kids it's their turn to do that with prefixes."

Hunn also finds that comics and cartoons can help a teacher observe students' development, and she cautions against cartoons built around racial slurs or profane or derogatory language, or those that remark about people or groups in a negative way.

WHY BOTHER?

There is a growing body of evidence that when humor is used in education and training:

- ** People absorb information more quickly;
- ** Many kinds of information are retained longer;
- ** There is a reduction in anxiety about subjects like math and science;
- ** There are fewer classroom management problems.

Kylene Norman and John Bailey of Clark Technical College in Springfield, Ohio, are engineering professors who show youngsters, in a tasty and humorous way, that mathematics can be fun and that computers don't have to be complicated. They know that many youngsters get turned off to math in middle or junior high school. Using a package of TicTac candies and a four-page guide with sample math problems, they "opened the possibility of eating one's mistakes." They added humor to their lectures with illustrated T-shirts. They have found weak students catching on to ideas both by listening and doing, and they have had students tell them that they like math class for the first time.

CLOWNING AROUND

Floppy-shoed, purple-haired Patches, along with other Ringling Bros. and Barnum & Bailey Circus clowns, promotes literacy. Using magic and clowning antics he shows young children that "Reading Lets You Imagine" and "Reading Lets You Learn." Look for Patches to visit elementary schools whenever the circus is in town. It is his way of giving something back to the community. Patches' pratfalls not only bring students guffaws, they stimulate a new excitement about reading.

HOW IMPORTANT IS A LAUGH?

A report in the Columbus, Ohio *Dispatch* detailed the search for a new Columbus Schools superintendent after the current superintendent had announced that he would not ask the Board of Education to renew his contract. The job was to be advertised and interviews to be conducted. The process, which took place in 1982, involved a committee of 40-50 members representing various parts of the community. They came up with a list of 50 qualities they wanted in a superintendent. Among the most important items on the list were: *has a sense of humor,* is tactful, anticipates problems, has budgetary skills, knows how to promote a positive and excellent climate.

DON'T BERATE 'EM, JOIN 'EM

So, teachers, why not join in with the healthy laughter of children? You probably could use a good laugh yourself and, by joining in, you become a role-model for healthy laughter. When the laughter in the classroom subsides you will all be more relaxed, you will have added a shared positive experience to your mutual history. Your morale and self-esteem will have been raised, and everyone left refreshed and ready to get back to work.

I find it encouraging that a great many teachers are interested in learning about humor. Think of what a tremendous difference it would make in the lives of children, in how they would feel about themselves, if all kids had teachers who tolerated, appreciated, and encouraged good-natured laughter, fun, and play.

49 PRACTICAL TEACHING IDEAS FOR PARENTS AND TEACHERS

Adapted with permission from *Learning Through Laughter: Humor in the Classroom,* by Claudia E. Cornett, Phi Delta Kappa Educational Foundation, Bloomington, Indiana, 1986.

1. Read aloud something humorous each day. Your library has a bibliography of humorous books. Shel Silverstein, Jack Plrelutsky, and William Coles have delightful poetry books. Robert Newton Peck's *Soup* books are great read-alouds for intermediate students. Nothing can beat Beverly Cleary for grades 2 to 4.

2. Start a humorous quotations collection to which students can add. They could be on a bulletin board or in a file box. *Bartlettts' Quotations* and other collections can be found in most libraries; many are organized by subject areas. [A wonderfully unique compendium of quotes and quips is Steve Wilson's *Eat Dessert First,* from Advocate Publishing Group.]

3. Organize a joke festival or marathon as a culmination of a language arts unit. Build up to it with a joke-of-the-week on the board or have a joke drop-box that students can read from when other work is complete.

4. Hold a best-joke contest. Have students rate submitted jokes or read them aloud to determine funniness rating.

5. Collect spoonerisms (for example, *It's kisstumary to cuss the bride*) and other humorous language forms: puns, pleonasms, conundrums, mixed idioms, palindromes, epitaphs, tall tales, tangletalk, chants, limericks, riddles, etc.

6. Do an art project with pictures of animal or body parts combined to create incongruous images. Have students name their creations.

7. Collect and then alphabetize into a class book all the words students can think of that describe ways to laugh and smile.

8. Do group creative writing using the word "laugh" as many times as possible. Student teams can compete, but their stories must make sense.

9. Share personal humorous anecdotes and allow students to do the same.

10. Compile a school "humor directory" that includes people's names and something humorous they can do or tell about to a class.

11. Analyze humorous literature for types of humor (for example, Amelia Bedelia taking things too literally).

12. For vocabulary development ask half the class to pantomime different smiles, while the other half guesses (for example, polite smile, grimace, grin, beam).

13. Put different laughs on cards, distribute them, and have students demonstrate (for example, guffaw, snicker, giggle, chortle, snort, cackle, chuckle).

14. Draw or pantomime nonliteral expressions (for example, shoplifting, cooking up a storm).

15. Parody television program titles or product names (for example, Crappy Days, Crust Toothpaste, Axwell House Coffee).

16. Make a chart of what makes people laugh: words, people, objects, events.

17. Create a funny "word wall" where students can tape up words such as zoot suit, bubble, burp.

18. Build a humorous learning center. See "Joke Center" in *Teacher* (March 1979) and "Limerick Center" in *Language Arts* (September 1976).

19. Have students keep a log of when and why they laugh.

20. Play tickle tag. Elementary students will enjoy tickling instead of tagging.

21. Do humor collages, for example, words, smiles, faces.

22. Collect humorous songs or songs that have something to do with humor and sing one a day, for example, "I Love to Laugh," "The Shadow of Your Smile," "When Irish Eyes are Smiling," "When You're Smiling," and "Smile Awhile." Don't forget favorite camp songs like "The Ole Gray Mare," "On Top of Old Smokey," "Mares Eat Oats," and "Bill Grogan's Goat."

23. Give each student a humor-related word to look up in a large dictionary to determine its etymology (for example, laugh, chortle, giggle, smirk).

24. Study the history and science of humor. Every encyclopedia has a section on humor.

25. Investigate the possibility of having a physician speak on the physical changes laughter produces. (More and more doctors are becoming interested in humor's healing powers.)

26. Put a humorous item on each test.

27. Find humorous art (for example, Mona Lisa parodies). Explain, discuss parody.

28. Collect laughs on a tape recorder. Label and try to match to owners.

29. Collect humorous quotations and photos from newspapers.

30. Listen to humorous records (for example, Bill Cosby).

31. Set up a tongue-twister station for students to use when work is complete. Have students practice and record times on a graph.

32. Start every Monday with something fun so students will look forward to coming to school, that is, BGIM (Be Glad It's Monday) instead of TGIF.

33. Use humorous sentences during spelling tests.

34. Practice punctuation by using unpunctuated jokes and limericks.

35. Have a backwards day. Run your schedule backwards, put some clothes on backwards, do last items on worksheets first, etc.

36. Have students research and then write biographies of comedians and authors of humorous works.

37. Take candid school shots with a camera and let students caption them.

38. Re-write fairy tales, myths, etc., in updated form.

39. Find humorous (safe) stunts that students can learn to do (for example, push potato across room with nose, roll eyes, wiggle ears, hambone rhythms).

40. Do creative writing or original riddles, jokes, tall tales, etc. (See *Journal of Reading*, March 1981 and *Reading Teacher*, 1982, for bibliographies.)

41. Learn signing of humor words as used by deaf people (for example, smile, laugh, etc.).

42. Study humor of different cultures and collect jokes and humorous stories from different countries.

43. Do a unit on humor using art, music, creative writing, speaking, listening, humorous literature.

44. Play a trick on the class each day by making something incongruous in the classroom that they must find.

45. Set up a display on humorous literature and authors in the library.

46. Have students collect and write "books" of Funny Family Folklore. Begin by having them ask parents, grandparents, and siblings to tell stories of funny things that happened to them.

47. Watch sitcoms and other television programs and list types and examples of humor used.

48. Invite a comedian to speak to the class about how he or she prepares material. Perhaps this could be coordinated with a career day.

49. Give the humor questionnaire below and share the results with the class.

FIND YOUR FUNNY BONE

a. Humor is____

b. On a 1 to 10 scale, my sense of humor is____________________
(Rate 10 as excellent and 1 as nonexistent.)

c. My favorite comedian/comedienne is________________________

d. ____is funny to me.

e. A funny thing that happened to me was______________________

f. I laughed until I cried when_______________________________

g. My laugh could be described as____________________________

h. ____________________________________has a memorable laugh.

i. ________________________________snorts when he or she laughs.

j. My favorite joke is______________________________________

k. I hate it when someone laughs when_________________________

l. People are funny who____________________________________

m. Babies are funny when___________________________________

n. A funny thing I heard a child say was_______________________

o. I am ticklish when______________________________________

p. The last time I blooped was_______________________________

q. I had to laugh at myself when_____________________________

r. ____makes me laugh.

CHAPTER 9

"PWLOARYKing YOUR LOVE LIFE"

Love may make the world go round but it's laughter that keeps us from getting dizzy.
--Donald Zochert

I kissed my first girl and smoked my first cigarette in the same day. I haven't had time for tobacco since. --Arturo Toscanini

Acting is not very hard. The most important things are to be able to laugh and to cry. If I have to cry, I think of my sex life. And if I have to laugh, well, I think of my sex life.
--Glenda Jackson

The most difficult years of marriage are those following the wedding. --Author unknown

A relationship without humor is like shaking hands with gloves on.
--Sherry Suib Cohen

Over the years I have addressed dozens of groups of singles and couples who are looking for answers to the eternal questions, "What do women want? What do men want?" The answers may be easier than some of our long, and sometimes loud, discussions would lead us to believe.

The over-abundance of books, articles, and TV "investigations" by Geraldo, Sally, Phil, Oprah, Barbara, Morton, Joan, Tom, Dick, and Harry have also failed to reveal the answer. There is some evidence that a successful long-term relationship takes work. You cannot take a relationship for granted, say many marriage counselors, you have to *work* at it. Well, anything which requires work presents us with an opportunity for PWLOARYK. We keep overlooking what is, perhaps, the single most important ingredient in successful intimacy: the sense of humor.

Let's look at the facts. *Glamour* magazine reported a survey of 350 brides-to-be who were asked what they admired most in their men. The quality most often mentioned: sense of humor (outranking romantic nature, intelligence, and good looks). Speaking for the sponsor of the study, Alice Kolator said, "These women take the decision to marry seriously. But the courtship has also got to be lighthearted."

Another fact. A *Newsweek* article reported that, in a study of 351 couples married 15 years or more, researchers Robert and Jeanette Lauer found that the most admired qualities in a spouse were integrity, caring, sensitivity, and a sense of humor.

WHAT DO THEY WANT?

One more fact. A report in *Men's Health* showed what a publishing company found when they tallied the attributes most frequently mentioned in its newsletter's personal ads. Humor topped the list for men and women alike. The results, published in *East/West Journal*, looked like this:

QUALITIES MOST OFTEN SOUGHT BY WOMEN IN MEN	QUALITIES MOST FREQUENTLY SOUGHT BY MEN IN WOMEN
1. Sense of humor	1. Sense of humor
2. Intelligence	2. Intelligence

3. Nonsmoker	3. Warmth
4. Sensitivity	4. Attractiveness
5. Being Committed	5. Nonsmoker
6. Being caring	6. Being slender
7. Being compassionate	7. Being sensitive
8. Attractiveness	8. Being caring
9. Warmth	9. Independence
10. Maturity	10. Honesty

Clearly, the report concluded, Sylvester Stallone is no match for Woody Allen in the rugged world of romance.

Because true mirthful laughter always discharges emotional tension, it helps you feel relaxed and is part of the "ice-breaker" people need when they first meet. As a relationship progresses, the partners will develop "in" jokes which help them feel special, draw them closer together, and reinforce their bonding. When the tough times come (and they will), a sense of humor will help again, by relieving tension and giving the couple a perspective from which they are less likely to be overwhelmed by their problems. "Intimate laughter," according to James Kaplan, writing for *MADEMOISELLE,* "is the laughter of people who've already found and accepted each other. Your love tickles you; you tickle him. The world tickles you both. It suffices."

. . . AND SEXY, TOO

"You can't be truly sexy if you are afraid of looking foolish in bed."

—Author unknown

Sex therapist Dr. Ruth Westheimer says, "In a relationship, if there's laughter from making fun of your partner, that's not always good. But if a joke is used to break tension, it can be very effective in defusing an explosive situation. For example, if a man gets mad because his girlfriend squeezes the toothpaste from the middle instead of the end, he shouldn't make a big scene. A little joke will help much more." Westheimer adds, "A sense of humor in bed can be very nice if used in the right way. But it can also be very dangerous. Some tickling or telling funny stories in bed can make sex more interesting." (This has to be the origin of "timing is everything!")

Writer Peter Mehlman says, "Without a sense of humor, life is the kind of thing that can leave a bad taste in your mouth." And, as Sherry Suib Cohen points out, "If you can count on a laugh, sometimes once a day, sometimes more, from your nearest and dearest, consider yourself blessed. I suspect that when we are old and gray we will remember the times we had each other in stitches far more vividly than the times we just had each other."

A FUNNY VALENTINE COULD BE SERIOUS

Pet names, private jokes, whimsical gifts, and shared fantasies are the games of love. In an extensive study, William Betcher, M.D., discovered that lighthearted play and humor can kindle, renew, and reaffirm romance, ease stressful situations, help solve problems, circumvent crises, and add excitement to our relationships. He maintains that humor is important not only for the pure pleasure it offers, but for the loving way it allows you to deal with trouble spots. You can read his fascinating findings in *Intimate Play: Playful Secrets For Falling And Staying In Love* (Penquin Books).

*Waltz her around the room while you hum her favorite song.

*Ask her what's the matter in your best Pee Wee Herman voice.

*Leave little surprise notes around the house for her, such as, in the freezer: "Honey, the meatloaf was great!" or, about 100 pages ahead of the bookmark in her bedside mystery: "I don't know whodunit, but I'd love to do it with you."

*Slip a new tape into her car stereo if she's been complaining about traffic jams on the way home.

*Carve a heart encircling your initials in the bar of soap she takes to the gym.

*Put a candy bar in her briefcase if you know she loves chocolate.

*Underneath the bread in the sandwich she takes for lunch: "I love you!"

From the first meeting to courtship, marriage, and beyond, it is apparent that a sense of humor and an element of playfulness is vital. However, if your sense of humor isn't enough to get you successfully all the way through the marriage phase, you can always employ it at the time of divorce. Not too long ago *Dear Abby* offered these examples of authentic divorce announcements:

SPLIT
After Six Years
Lester and Betty
Have seen the light
Married November 8, 1966
Divorced November 6, 1972
Both are happily back in circulation.
Call Lester: 555-6500 (After 9 p.m.)
Betty: 555-1115 (anytime)

* * *

WITH HAPPY HEARTS
Lionel and Jane announce with pleasure
the severance of all legal
and/or other bonds that may have
existed between their daughter

Janet and That Boy
With the new month of August
Janet enters into a new and
beautiful single life

As for That Boy--May the Great
Honcho in the sky love him and
Keep him--someplace else

Clearly, improving your laugh life will improve--or save--your love life, make you more attractive, and bring satisfaction to your intimate relationships. Here is my best tip for a happy marriage: my wife and I try to maintain a sense of humor about our marriage: I don't try to run her life, and I don't try to run mine, either. That works out real well! (As a marriage counselor, I have been able to draw on the work of people like Alan King, Henny Youngman, and Erma Bombeck where I find many good reminders about the importance of a humorous perspective in love and marriage.)

CHAPTER 10

"SO YOU CANT TELL A JOKE"

There is an increasing awareness that humor and laughter are good for us, and most of us want to get all the goodies we can. Oscar Wilde went so far as to proclaim, "Pleasure is the only thing to live for" and, according to Sebastian Chamfort, "The most wasted day is that in which we have not laughed." Every day there is more evidence of the ability of humor and laughter to heal us physically, mentally, emotionally, and spiritually. Every system of the body responds to laughter in some positive, healing way. Leo Rosten warns, "I hope you are not foolish enough to consider humor insignificant and dismiss jokes as 'trivia'."

One big problem with jokes is that most of us have neither good "joke memories" nor good joke telling abilities. In fact, a very few people can tell jokes well. Perhaps as a result of listening to your brother-in-law's attempts, you already know that. I have repeatedly surveyed the thousands of participants at my humor PLAYSHOP LABS and the audiences at my speeches for their joke-telling ability. In spite of the fact that about 90% of them feel that they have a good sense of humor, only about 2% feel they can tell a joke really well. The vast majority also admit that they can't think of a snappy comeback when someone hits them with a "zinger," until about two hours (or two *days*) later, when they have the flash of insight, "Now I know what I should have said to him!!" By then, of course, it's too late.

Not to worry.

Everyone can locate and develop their sense of humor. Many people mistakenly limit themselves by believing that, when it comes to a sense of humor, "either you've got it or you don't." NOT TRUE! What is true, however, is that the ability to laugh and smile are inborn--the neurological substrates for laughing and smiling are mature at birth in human infants. But this is not the same thing as having a sense of humor. As Annette Goodheart, Ph.D., points out, when an infant laughs in its crib we don't rush over and say, "That kid's got a great sense of humor." Laughter is a natural mechanism for, among other things, discharging emotional tension. In fact, a Jewish proverb states, "What soap is to the body, laughter is to the soul."

Laughter is irrational, which means "without reason." It is a way of being temporarily out of control which happens to have some very pleasant and beneficial effects. You do not need a reason to laugh. In fact, if you stop to examine the reason you are laughing, you will probably kill the laughter.

There is reasoning, intellect, or cognitive ability associated with some forms of humor because they require assessment, judgement, and imagination. Rita Mae Brown wrote, "Wit comes from intellect, humor comes from emotion, and fun comes from imagination." I would add that, often, laughter erupts reflexively or from the element of surprise. We all have times when we laugh and we can't explain why. The next time someone asks, "What's so funny?" don't feel obligated to come up with an answer.

So, you can't tell a joke and you still want to share humor with friends, business associates, co-workers, customers, and loved-ones? Here are ten ideas for experiencing more humor, and inviting warm feelings, smiles, chuckles, and even guffaws, without ever having to tell a joke:

1. Look for the unintended humor of reality and collect examples in a notebook or file to share with others or just to review yourself whenever you need a lift. Sample: A sign seen in a Bangkok dry cleaners, "Drop your trousers here for best results."

2. Wear funny T-shirts. Have "Funny T-shirt day" at work. My wife, Pam, especially likes one that carries the message, "A Husband Is Living Proof That A Wife Can Take A Joke!"

3. Become a toy-aholic. You never outgrow your need for toys as a way to induce playfulness and laughter. Make it a point to shop for toys for yourself. Buy the toy that suits you best. Whether it's a simple wind-up toy that can move across your desk or an elaborate electronic gizmo, if it brings a smile to your face, it will give you the humor break you need to ward off the ill-effects of stress. Or it may be just the ice-breaker you need to get to know a new employee or customer.

4. Wear fun buttons. These are available almost anywhere. Start your own collection. Some of my favorites are, "I'm not deaf. I'm ignoring you!" and "Enjoy life! This is not a dress rehearsal." The button conveys the humor, so you don't have to tell a joke.

5. Hang up humor. One easy way is to put cartoons on bulletin boards at work. Or put up a humorous poster in your office, at your desk, or in your locker. When there are cartoons on bulletin boards, people will read more of the other notices. When your eye catches a funny poster you get a lightening quick way to lighten up.

6. Schedule time for humor. Be sure you get to see that favorite funny T.V. show, go to a comedy club, or just take time to play. With today's busy schedules, it's important to put "fun time" on the calendar and make is "sacred time," not to be postponed.

7. Enroll in a humor class. Many adult education programs are now offering classes designed to help you discover and develop your humorous personality. Several types of "Humor Conventions" and conferences are now held throughout the year nationally and internationally. GO!

8. Hang out with people who make you laugh or people who have a well-developed sense of humor. If you know people who leave you feeling tense, drained, guilty, depressed, or otherwise bummed-out, don't hang around them! Spend time with people who leave

9. Subscribe to humorous periodicals. Have you heard of "Laughter Works," "Laughing Matters," "Current Comedy," "The Jokesmith," "The Steve Wilson Report," or "The Journal of Polymorphous Perversity"? These go beyond *MAD* magazine (which is good, too). All of them are not necessarily funny but they will help you find your funnybone.

10. Become a Humor Penpal and exchange humor with people from all over the world via mail and FAX. See *The Last Word,* page 137, for details.

Use these ideas and find others that work to help you be more humorous, and less serious, and get the most out of life. Remember, everything goes better with humor, and you definitely do not have to tell jokes to prove it.

CHAPTER 11

CELEBRATE SOMETHING DIFFERENT FOR A CHANGE

In Chapter 4, many of the examples of having fun at work involved celebration of some kind: a job well done, a birthday, anniversary, or a holiday. Almost all of the celebration ideas which were submitted had themes based on the standard holidays such as Valentine's Day or Christmas. A few of the celebration ideas were more inventive, which gave me the idea of finding even more reasons to celebrate, especially among the offbeat-but-officially-proclaimed events.

Celebration creates a shared festive experience which adds to the positive history of the work group. Enjoying these playful experiences together provides the balance needed for the heavy stresses of the day. Being able to recall these experiences later is a powerful way of boosting morale and cohesiveness.

You can brighten up your office or department (or even your home) by finding ways to celebrate the following special events. While you're at it, why not invent your own special days? Every once in a while, have a "There's Nothing To Celebrate" celebration. (Whenever you come across a bona fide special day, send it along to me and I'll add it to the list.)

JANUARY:

-National Hobby Month
-Trivia Day (4th)
-Sherlock Holmes' Birthday
-Zanzibar Revolution Day (Tanzania)
-National Nothing Day (16th)
-National Hugging Day (21st)
-National Prune Breakfast Month
-National Pizza Week (15th-22nd)
-National Kazoo Day (28th)
-National Popcorn Day (Superbowl Sunday)

FEBRUARY:

-American Heart Month
-Bean Throwing Festival (Setsubun, Japan)
-Waitangi Day (New Zealand)
-Mary Queen of Scots Execution Anniversary (1587)
-Boy Scouts of America Anniversary (8th)
-French Fry Day (4th Friday)
-Dan Quayle's Birthday (2/4/47)
-Ferris Wheel Day (Birth anniversary of George Ferris, 1889)
-National Pancake Week (10th-16th)
-Independence Day - Estonia (24th)
-Bun Day - Iceland (26th)
-Bubba Smith's Birthday (b 1945)

MARCH:

-National Pig Day (1st)
-Texas Independence Day (2nd)
-National Procrastination Week (4th-10th)
-National Peanut Month
-National Nutrition Month
-National Frozen Food Month
-Bang Clang Day (9th)
-Fun Mail Week (8th-14th)
-Buzzard's Day - Hinckley, Ohio (15th)
-National Goof Off Day (22nd)
-Pecan Day (25th)
-Bunsen Burner Day (31st)

APRIL:

-St. Lasarus Day - Bulgaria (1st)
-Sorry, Charlie Day (1st Saturday)
-Week of The Young Child (5th-11th)
-World Health Day (7th)
-Commodore Perry Day (10th)
-Barbershop Quartet Day (11th)
-Professional Speakers Day (12th)
-Swallow Day - San Juan Capistrano (15th)
-Dismal Day (20th)
-Birthday of Rome (753 B.C.)
-National Anxiety Month
-World Cow Chip Throwing Championship (21st-28th)

MAY:

-American Bike Month
-Better Sleep Month
-National Barbecue Month
-Lumpy Rug Day (3rd)
-International Tuba Day (1st Friday)
-No Socks Day (8th)
-Mental Health Month
-National High Blood Pressure Month
-National Nurses Day (6th)
-Bob Marley Day - Jamaica (11th)
-Trini Lopez Birthday (b. 1937)
-Public Relations Week (last full week)

JUNE:

-Zoo & Aquarium Month
-National Ragweed Control Month
-Yell "Fudge" at the Cobras in North America Day (2nd)
-Donut Day (1st)
-National Yo-Yo Day (6th)
-Organic Act Day - Virgin Islands (18th)
-Jane Russell's Birthday (21st, b. 1921)
-National Tennis Week (June 20-28)
-Captain Kangaroo's Birthday (27th, b. 1927)
-Family Day (1st Sunday)

JULY:

-National Baked Bean Month
-National Hot Dog Month
-National Anti-Boredom Month
-Disobedience Day (3rd)
-American Redneck Day (4th)
-O.J. Simpson's Birthday (9th, b. 1947)
-Be Nice To New Jersey Week (8th - 14th)
-National Cheer Up The Lonely Day (11th)
-National Nudist Day (16th)
-Take Your Houseplants For A Walk Day (27th)
-Birthday of the Singing Telegram (28th, 1933)

AUGUST:

-National Catfish Month
-Lizzie Borden Liberation Day (4th)
-National Mustard Day (5th)
-Mata Hari's Birthday (7th, b. 1876)
-Jimmy Dean's Birthday (10th, b. 1928)
-National Relaxation Day (15th)
-National Aviation Day (19th)
-Vesuvius Day - Italy (24th)
-National Neighborhood Day (29th)

SEPTEMBER:

-Sight Saving Month
-Newspaper Carrier Day (4th)
-Be Late For Something Day (5th)
-Grandma Moses' Birthday (7th, b. 1860)
-National Boss/Employee Exchange Day (10th)
-Blame Someone Else Day (13th)
-National Anthem Day - Maryland (14th)
-Sophia Loren's Birthday (20th, b. 1934)
-National One-Hit Wonder Day (25th)
-National Laundry Week (21st-27th)
-National Good Neighbor Day (27th)

OCTOBER:

-National Liver Awareness Month
-National Popcorn Poppin Month
-World Vegetarian Day (1st)
-Ten-Four Day - Radio Operators (4th)
-Grandparents Day (7th)
-Leif Erikson Day (9th)
-National School Lunch Week (begins 2nd Sunday)
-Be Bald And Be Free Day (14th)
-National Grouch Day (15th)
-TV Talk Show Host Day (23rd)
-National Magic Week (25th-31st)

NOVEMBER:

-National Notary Public Week (the full week containing Nov. 7th)
-National Sandwich Day (3rd)
-Saxophone Day (6th)
-National Notary Public Day (7th)
-Rodin's Birthday (12th, b. 1840)
-National Children's Book Week (16th-22nd)
-Homemade Bread Day (17th)
-Mickey Mouse's Birthday (18th)
-Buffalo Bob (Smith's) Birthday (27th, b. 1917)
-National Family Week (22nd-28th)

DECEMBER:

-Christmas . . . Chanukah . . . Skiing season beings . . . First Day of Winter . . . New Year's Eve
-Ozzy Osbourne's Birthday (3rd, b. 1948)
-National Roof Over Your Head Day (10th)
-Bill of Rights Day (15th)
-Underdog Day (21st)
-Feast of the Radishes (23rd)
-Humphrey Bogart's Birthday (25th, b. 1899)

CHAPTER 12

BULLETIN BOARD BRIGHTENERS

How can you tell if a place of business is practicing PW-LOARYK? One of the first things I do when I walk into any workplace is to look for signs of life through the humor on the employee bulletin board. This is an easy place to inject some lightness with excellent results. It is especially important for me to take note of this opportunity for communication in businesses for which I am the humor consultant.

Some of these bulletin boards are really dull. How much more boring can you get than to have the extreme uniformity of every notice posted on the exact same size paper with the exact same color thumb tacks placed exactly the same distance from each corner of each sheet of paper? Do managers really expect that boring, bland notices will attract attention?

My recommendation is to include some color and some humor on bulletin boards for maximum attractiveness. In fact, if you set aside a corner of the bulletin board and reserve it for the "jokes of the week," people will come around to see the new jokes and that means you get another opportunity to get them reading the notices with the information that you want them to have.

There are zillions of wonderful jokes, posters, stories, signs, poems, and cartoons which are part of the urban folklore known as "office copier humor." What office doesn't have at least a few employees who have a secret stash of these wonderful gags and funnies? The examples I have seen range from hilarious and clean to crude, sexist, racist, and triple-X-rated. I have an extensive collection myself and it grows every week with the examples that are mailed and faxed to me by humor penpals across the country. There are even books on office copier humor, giving you loads of funny things to copy and pass around.

Here are some bulletin board brighteners you can run through the office copier and post for the enjoyment of all (and to get them reading the messages). The copyright is waived as long as you don't sell the material.

DO YOU WANT
TO TALK TO THE
MAN
IN CHARGE, OR
THE
WOMAN
WHO KNOWS
WHAT'S GOING
ON?

Sure God created Man before Woman but then you always make a rough draft before the . . .

FINAL MASTERPIECE

NOTICE

THIS PLACE REQUIRES

NO PHYSICALFITNESS PROGRAM.

EVERYONE GETS ENOUGH EXERCISE

JUMPING TO CONCLUSIONS,

FLYING OFF THE HANDLE,

RUNNING DOWN THE BOSS,

KNIFING FRIENDS IN THE BACK,

DODGING RESPONSIBILITY

AND

PUSHING THEIR LUCK!

GOD . . .

I Love This Place!

but . . .

Please be patient

with me.

I only work here

because . . .

CHAPTER 13

THE SENSES OF HUMOR

It has been said, "There are very few good judges of humor, and they don't agree." Yes, hard as it is to believe, not everyone likes Peanuts.

Have you ever been the only person laughing out loud during a movie? Do you sometimes find yourself to be the only one laughing at jokes, situations, comedians, or comic strips? Do other people sometimes wonder about your weird sense of humor? Has someone come up to you to tell you that you are about to hear their funniest joke, but after hearing it, you don't get the humor? And after they control their own hysterical laughter long enough to explain the joke to you, are you still in the dark, as if they know something that you don't?

Fear not! You are not humor impaired or punch-line deficient. Even though you always suspected that you do have a sense of humor, you and your friend probably just don't share the same "sense" of humor. As Shakespeare put it, "A jest's prosperity lies more in the ear of the listener than in the mouth of the speaker." In other words, it's different jokes for different folks.

Fortunately, there are hundreds, maybe thousands of different "senses" of humor. What tickles your funnybone won't necessarily tickle mine. That is as it should be.

What a boring world it would be if we all had the same sense of humor. There would be only one cartoon in the Sunday funnies, one sitcom on TV, and one comedian to make the round of all the talk shows and comedy clubs. And we would have only one type of joke--or, worse yet, only one joke! "Did you hear the one about . . . " "Yes, yes, yes. I've heard it a thousand times!!!"

You and I probably don't have the same favorite comic strip or cartoon character, TV sitcom, comedian, or humorous author. The point is we don't have to like the same things. Just as tastes differ in many things, they differ with humor, too. What you find funny, I may not. What I find laughable, you may not. Here is a partial alphabetical list of senses of humor. Can you locate yours?

Abstract, amusing, antic, bawdy, buffoon, bumpkin, bizarre, child-like, clever, cornball, cheerful, cynical, daring, darling, deadpan, devilish, derisive, droll, dry, elfish, expansive, facetious, farcical, far-out, flaky, gleeful, gross, grotesque, hostile, hysterical, impish, insulting, jocular, jolly, jovial, kibitzing, licentious, lively, ludicrous, merry, mischievous, nitwit, nonsensical, observational, off-beat, outrageous, parody, perverse, playful, poor-soul, punny, quirky, raucous, ribald, risque, sarcastic, sardonic, satirical, self-deprecating, sick, silly, simple, smart-alec, superior, teasing, topical, uninhibited, unique, vexatious, visual, wacky, waggish, weird, whimsical, witty, wry, x-rated, yummy, zany.

PEACE THROUGH HUMOR

I believe we can promote world peace and harmony through humor. In a free society we have choices; we can express our preferences in humor by enjoying the humor we find personally satisfying. Gerald Ford, a President who needed a sense of humor and who, incidentally, used it very effectively, said, "Unlike freedom of the press, laughter is not specifically protected by an amendment to our Constitution. Nevertheless, it is probably the clearest and most resounding expression of freedom we have." Roseanne Barr says stand-up comedy is the last free-expression art-form left in the country.

Perhaps one of the most important ways humor can promote world peace is by promoting tolerance for the fact that there are many different senses of humor and one is not better or more important than any of the others. They are merely different. And, as Jim Boren points out, "Though a humorist may bomb occasionally, it is still better to exchange humorists than bombs. And . . . you can't fight when you're laughing." Psychologist and public speaker par excellence, Dr. Herb True says, "If you can find anything to laugh about when you are angry, you won't stay angry as long."

If we could learn to appreciate differences in senses of humor, we could increase tolerance generally, and decrease hostility in the world. The next time you hear a joke or story that someone else finds humorous, and you don't get it, try to see it as an opportunity to enjoy the richness and variety of human experience and tastes. Don't put the other person down. Appreciate that we are all different, and those differences represent not threats, but valuable resources. But, be careful of using humor to ridicule or diminish the value of another person's culture, beliefs, or appearance. We need less judgmentalism in this world. Critical people who sit in judgement of others cause more emotional problems than anything else I know. I treat these problems in my office every day.

Even humor which is in questionable taste has a usefulness. Gene Shalit says, "Goodhearted ethnic humor in America has largely vanished. Too bad for America." I agree. And I would underscore that what has been lost is our "goodhearted" attitude, leaving us with fear-based and narrow-minded ethnic jokes which demean others and perpetuate unfortunate stereotypes. (What do you think most people associate with "Polish"?)

Educator Max J. Herzberg advised that, "One who wishes to cultivate a sense of humor must learn that there are times, at least, when he must free himself from dignity, restraint, and prejudice, and be ready for the great pretenses of play." Humor which some would find objectionable often allows us to cope with otherwise impossible situations. Mel Brooks tells us, "Humor is the last defense against the universe." And through humor, one can raise issues that you would not otherwise bring up. Throughout the ages, those who are oppressed have used humor to reduce their oppressors to a psychologically more manageable size. Joking about anything that oppresses us makes it less frightening. I remember that, during World War II, when I was a young boy, there was a proliferation of cartoon caricatures depicting Mussolini, Hirohito, and Hitler. They somehow gave us a feeling of superiority over our enemies.

Bill Dana and Laurence Peter, in their book *The Laughter Prescription*, make a convincing case that "from the loss of a loved one to the loss of your hair, humor can help you cope with anything." Humor defuses angry situations, discharges emotional tension, helps us to be more attractive, persuasive, likeable, creative, productive, relaxed, communicative, and healthy. I can't imagine getting all those benefits if we had only one joke, only one comic-strip cartoon, and only one TV sitcom. We benefit most when there is a great variety of humor to appeal to all tastes and needs.

There are opportunities at work for spontaneous joking and laughter. If you have been present when it happened, you know that the unplanned humor helped to relieve a tense situation. But there are principles which you can intentionally apply in order to be sure that you get the greatest benefits from mixing work and play.

So, you tickle your funnybone and I'll tickle mine and if we both laugh at the same things, that's great; if we don't laugh at the same things, that's great, too! After all, it truly is different jokes for different folks!

THE LAST WORD

HUMOR PENPALS

Over the years I have become an informal clearing house for humor through a network called Humor Penpals.

By becoming a Humor Penpal you have the opportunity to swap humor with people all over North America. There is no fee for this but you must make an in-kind humor contribution. The way to do this is to mail anything which you find humorous (a cartoon, newspaper headline, anecdote, greeting card, bumper sticker, office-copier jokes, etc.) to:

Humor Penpals
c/o Steve Wilson
Suite 120
3400 N. High Street
Columbus, OH 43202.

Or FAX the same funny material to 614-263-LAFF.

When you mail in your humor contribution, you will be guaranteed in return a generous sampling of what other Humor Penpals have sent, IF you send along a self-addressed-stamped envelope. FAXed contributions merit FAXed humor in return.

A CERTIFIED SENSE OF HUMOR

If you have a way of mixing work and play which was not included in the list in Chapter 3, send it to the above address, and two wonderful things will happen.

(1) Your idea will eventually be shared with thousands of other people who need encouragement and suggestions for PWLOARYKing and,

(2) You will receive an official "Sense of Humor" certificate, IF you send along a self-addressed-stamped envelope.

Thanks for joining in the fun!